GOING HOME GROWN UP

"*Going Home Grown Up* opens up a common challenge with uncommon grace and wisdom. I think of members of my own family who could find it extraordinarily helpful. Anne Grizzle enriches us with stories from her own life experience and faith in God who, as she says, 'must fill our deepest wells.'"
    Leighton Ford
    Leighton Ford Ministries

"Anne Grizzle is a wise and realistic counselor. Many people who need this book will be blessed by it."
    Harold S. Kushner

"Anne Grizzle has written a real winner of a book! I often feel I regress from 54 to 14 years old, driving up the driveway to my parents' house. I am 8 by the time the door opens and 3 for the rest of the visit. Anne has a beautiful guidebook on how to stay grown up around your parents. I can hardly wait to practice it this Christmas! I am recommending this book to all my clients."
    Newton Hightower, LMSW-ACP, President
    Houston Association for Marriage and Family Therapy

"Anne Grizzle's way with words, her creative images, and her personal examples come together to invite the reader to make the most of his or her family relationships while there is time. I found myself remembering with fondness family stories I had forgotten and challenging myself to return to places that need further exploring."
    Winnie Honeywell
    Director of Catholic Family Life Ministry

"If you have ever felt anger, discomfort, frustration, or pain in relationships with your parents or siblings, Anne Grizzle's new book may change your life. It is by turns wise, moving, funny, and, most importantly, helpful. Be prepared for a psychological sea change in how you feel about and relate to your family of origin."
    The Very Reverend Ken Swanson, Ph.D., Dean and Rector
    Christ Church Cathedral, Nashville

Going Home Grown Up

A Relationship Handbook for Family Visits

Anne F. Grizzle

Harold Shaw Publishers
Wheaton, Illinois

Scripture quotations are taken from The New King James Version. Copyright © 1979, 1980, 1982, Thomas Nelson Inc., Publishers.

ISBN 0-87788-232-0

Cover design and illustration by David LaPlaca

Library of Congress Cataloging-in-Publication Data
Grizzle, Anne F., 1955-
  Going home grown up : a relationship handbook for family visits /
by Anne F. Grizzle.
      p.   cm.
  Includes bibliographical references (p.   ).
  ISBN 0-87788-232-0
    1. Parent and adult child. 2. Intergenerational relations.
  3. Interpersonal relations. I. Title.
  HQ755.86.G75   1998
  306.874—dc21   98-27540
                                                    CIP

03 02 01 00 99 98
10 9 8 7 6 5 4 3 2 1

To Betsy, Diane, Heidi, Sherry, and Adeline,
with deep gratitude for their companionship
on my journey

Contents

Acknowledgments

My special thanks . . .

To Joan, who through persistent belief in this book persuaded me to write it.

To my mother, father, sisters, and extended family, who have loved me through my growing up.

To my husband, who has enthusiastically and practically supported my creative endeavors.

To Sally, Deborah, Quita, Sharron, Kathleen, Cora, Beth, and Molly, who have personally helped and prayed me through my year of writing.

To all those who have allowed me the privilege of accompanying them on their home journeys (whose names and identities have been changed for the sake of confidentiality when mentioned in the book).

Introduction

I grew up visiting grandparents at a farm called Broadview, set amidst the rolling hills of the Shenandoah Valley. My grandfather had purchased the original piece of land with its old stone house when my mother was a girl, though only after she was grown did they make it their main home. My sisters and I loved playing tag with cousins in the barn hay bales, riding horses over the fox hound trails, and eating Granny's home-grown sweet corn every August. At the end of an active day, we would collapse around the heavily laden dinner table listening to my grandfather's stories of growing up in west Texas, secretly hopping a train for southwest Virginia, courting my grandmother on horseback, and then eloping with her. Granny and GrandPop's house at Broadview was one of my favorite places on earth. My parents spent relatively little time there, though they usually dropped me and my sisters off for long summer visits.

Interesting changes began when my grandfather died and left a piece of that family farm to my mother. My sisters and I were grown by then and living away from Virginia, but I began to read in my mother's letters about my parents going over to this spot of earth, carting rocks to fill in the road, laboring to cut wayward cedars, and rejoicing with thrashed thistles. They bought a little camping trailer, put it on a back corner, and named it the Homestead, providing them an outpost to facilitate their coming and working there more often. My parents began to spend a lot more time with my Uncle Jim and Aunt Kitty, as well as with other family members. They began doing what I think my grandfather had dreamed of their doing for years—loving the land and the family.

My parents have described to me the inner movement that happens when you own your own land and are responsible for it. They gained a new sense of connection; they realized that they had control and could make choices; they assumed responsibility; and they developed the property in new ways. They began to occupy the land, not just to play on it but to work it . . . and hard.

I believe that this same inner movement happens with our emotional and relational land, specifically the territory of connectedness with our family that we bring into our adulthood. As long as we feel that the activities and relationships that compose coming home involve merely a treading on our parents' territory—in which we have no real ownership or adult partnership—we will only visit. We will keep a certain physical and emotional distance. We may admire, critique, or marginally contribute but will probably not fully enjoy or work the land of family relationships.

As adults we often develop a sense of ownership in our own marriages and with our children. We feel and act grown up (at least most of the time). But on visits to see our parents, we revert to patterns of childhood. We fail to speak up for ourselves as adults or creatively work for growth. Instead, we passively or reactively endure for a time a return to the old-world ways. We forfeit any sense of ownership, with its concomitant sense of responsibility and possibility, regarding our family of origin and, hence, our visits home.

This book is about our taking ownership for our visits home to see parents and family, acting like grown-ups with the people who knew us as children. This requires preparing for our visits in new, relational ways. The hard work includes cutting down the annoying cedars of thoughtless activities and digging out the thistles of frustrating relationship patterns. The invitation includes clearing new roads in the form of new patterns and rituals for our family. This "homework" takes place on three levels. Section One will offer help for the first level: preparing specific, practical steps for improving the relational encounters of family visits. Even small steps can make perceptible changes in the difficult repeating scenarios of family interaction and contribute toward positive relationship growth. Section Two will explore the deeper, underlying work of transforming our core relationship roles: helping pampered children take more responsibility, heroes become more human, and victims gain voices. Finally, Section Three will challenge readers to use the lessons from their families in the work of creating their own new homes.

Changing patterns that we have acted out since we were born is a great challenge. Doing that with the very people who taught us those steps is even harder. But as adults we must do that, attending carefully to what we treasure as well as what we wish to change about our family relationships. If we do that personal "homework," we will claim emotional territory that we can enjoy together with our parents or family before they, or we, die. I invite you to dig into the soil of your family frustrations, to plow the way for better family visits, renewed relationships, and your own personal growth.

Chapter 1

Go Home without Shrinking

A strange thing happens when we return as adults to visit our parents. We may be six-feet, four-inches tall, president of a company and master of our home universe, but as our car turns down their block, our feet cross the threshold of their house, or our ears hear their voices, we suddenly shrink down to the size and role we were years ago when we were growing up as their children. I know a singer whose voice fills the sanctuary and touches hearts until eyes moist over but who can hardly get out a word of her true feelings when she visits her mother. I've seen a teacher of teens at an after-school community center revert to the defensive, screaming little brother with his older sister during a family reunion. A competent mother of three becomes the quiet daughter again, obedient to all her mother's prescribed solutions during the family Thanksgiving gathering. A law-school student becomes the awkward Little League player overshadowed by his tough older brother during family weekends at the beach. A businesswoman who has learned to balance her life moves right back into the imbalanced heroine role at Christmas, taking care of all the details and everyone's requests for a perfect holiday.

Slipping into Roles

When I was growing up, my family had a funny prayer that we would occasionally say, much to the amusement of guests. My father would begin with a deep, solemn "Lord, have mercy on our souls." My older sister would say softly with disdain, "Don't you dare touch those rolls!" followed by my nastily whispered "Be still. I see your feet" and my twin sister's defensive, "Don't you try that trick again." My mother, acting oblivious to what had gone on, would conclude, "Grant us peace and joy," and we would all chime in cheerfully, "Amen." Its simple, silly lines actually say much about the difficulty of mixing faith and family life in an honest way as well as the often double lives of our families. Thirty years later, sitting around a family dinner table, when my father says his line, all three adult daughters can chime in with their childish lines as if it were yesterday. And just as easily, we can slip into our roles as compliant, successful daughters, subtly but fiercely competitive sisters, and polite, don't-ever-get-angry churchgoers.

When we visit our family, our feelings and behaviors can shrink almost as clearly as the kids do physically in the movie *Honey, I Shrunk the Kids*. We slip into old roles just as we put on a well-worn pair of jeans or endure a repeating nightmare. Like actors coming back every summer to repeat a familiar theater piece, we take our cues, act our parts, and repeat our lines. The shrinking feeling is most pronounced when we return after some time away to visit parents, especially when we visit them on old home territory. However, the suction back into earlier emotional reactions and patterns of relating can occur any time we have contact with the people we lived with in our formative, growing-up years. So when Dad walks in the front door or Mom calls on the phone or we spend a day with our brother, we might find ourselves suddenly reacting in old ways. At holidays, this suction can be particularly powerful with the added weight of family traditions. The pull can be compounded for unmarried adults, as parents tend to treat singles even more like kids regardless of age. Our job hours may be expanding, our hair graying, or our résumé growing, but the old family patterns all too often remain the same, year after year, visit after visit.

The suction is powerful, the fit familiar. But we pay a high price when we give in without a plan. Our growing adult selves and souls are stifled (and hidden from those who should know them best). And our relationships become stuck and stale rather than genuine and growing. With our family we can begin to feel more like robots or actors than living, loving humans. We can lose the vibrancy of real relationships where individual adults interact honestly and creatively.

When we were children, adults frequently asked us what we wanted to be when we grew up. Answers ranged from fireman to teacher to animal tamer, depending on the day or our mood. Being grown up symbolized in our minds then, as well as now, the sense of having a choice in our own destiny, responsibility to act like an adult, and opportunity to try new things. This sense of being a grown-up is what we must bring into our home visits if we are to transform them from lifeless repetition of old problems and pains into opportunities for relational and personal growth. Age twenty-five or fifty rather than age twelve is perhaps the time to particularly heed the admonition to "act your age." Only by resisting the tendency to shrink back to old roles, taking initiative to plan our family visits, and nurturing our adult hopes for growth will we make our visits home memorable not for their catastrophes but for their connections.

> *for personal reflection*
>
> *In what ways do you shrink when you visit your family?*

Family is the hardest place to act our age, yet when we can be our true adult selves there, we have most fully come into our own. No one can rouse our anger, hurt, or frustration more deeply than family members. So when we deal with these emotions and relationships, we have dealt with our core. As the song says of New York City, if you can make it there, you can make it anywhere. Although we search the world over, there usually is also no one we would more value having a loving, honest, growing relationship with than our families.

Home Roots in Our Soul

Shortly after my second wedding anniversary, when my husband and I were living in New York, we prepared for a Thanksgiving trip to see my parents in Virginia. As I was talking about going home, he caught me up short and said rather pointedly, "This is your home now." He meant not so much New York but this marriage. I was (and still am) happily married, but I must confess neither our labored-over first apartment nor the arms of the man who adored me had yet become the place in my heart I called home. I have never again referred to trips to see my family as going home. But in my gut I still feel, as many people do, a sense of home when I return not so much to the beloved Virginia soil on which I ran as a child but to my mother and my father, the people who bore me, rocked me, and raised me.

Our first home remains in some senses forever an emotional home base for us all. In the bosom of our earthly mother and the hands of our earthly father we first learn about love and about relationships. Those breasts and hands may have nourished us well, giving us forever a wish to return to the safe haven of parental care. Or they may have been well-meaning but rather blundering. Or they may have been openly hostile and abusive. Yet from their flesh we learned what we know of relationships. These people who held us when we cried in the night, who watched us take our first steps and march off to kindergarten, who wept or yelled when we broke the window with the baseball, who clapped for us when we finally graduated from grade school or graduate school . . . they mold us and shape us, and even after we leave them we take their form and their voices with us.

Why Do You Go Home?

All of us return home to this family periodically throughout our lives. Some yearn to live with their parents forever (and a few actually do). Some live down the street or just across town, maybe even working together in a family business. Others have left the nest but return as often as possible from their active forays in the world, whether that involves a flight across continents or a walk down the block. Still others return regularly but less often, trying to keep a sometimes precarious balance between their own adult lives and staying in touch with family. A few return only rarely, yet still do so if only once a year out of guilt or once a decade for a family wedding or funeral. Or perhaps periodically, when hidden hope builds up, they go home just to see if perhaps things will have changed, to see if their parents will have come to their senses and will finally be able to give them the word or hug or look of affirmation they seek. Finally, a few are cut off completely from their parents because they have given up on them or their parents are no longer alive. Yet even these adult children still return if only in their minds to the hoped-for relationships of an original parental loving home. What does your relationship with your parents look like? And when you return, what are the reasons for your visit? Your reasons might include the following.

To Find Personal Support
When parents or grandparents, aunts or uncles have provided a warm nest and home base from which to launch out into the world, adult children often return home for a personal recharge. They may be annoyed by their parents' habits or embarrassed by their styles, but they know that their parents will love and delight in them. By virtue of their love and trust, these parents provide their children with a refueling of energy and hope for life.

To Honor Elders
Other adult children return home more out of duty. Sometimes this comes from the underlying cultural sense that you are supposed to keep up with your family. For those of faith, honoring father and mother is a core calling. This is the only command-

ment of the Old Testament ten with a specific con-
sequence, "that your days may be long upon the land
which the Lord your God is giving you" (Exodus
20:12). Inherent in living out a faith that values human lives and relationships is honoring those who
have brought you into the world and given you their
best, however great or paltry that might be.

To Seek Grandparents

Some adults go their way independently of their
parents. They are glad to get away and eager to seek
their own fortune. However, in the later seasons of
their lives, they return to family. Like parents returning to church out of concern for their children's
souls even though they have long since abandoned
regard for their own, adults often realize that their
children need grandparents in spite of their feeling
no need for parents themselves. Even adults who
believe their parents are awful are sometimes able
to salvage some good, like the wise woman who
despises her divorced husband but still encourages
her children to look for his good traits. Or adults
may admit that people do mellow with age, and the
harsh father may emerge a more tolerant grandfather
or the strict mother who made her five children
straighten their rooms like army recruits may grant
a granddaughter a reprieve to pile her toys in the
living room.

To Help Ailing Parents

The day usually comes for adult children when even
those who have been most occupied in pursuits
elsewhere are needed back at home. When Mom has
a stroke or Dad loses his job, trips home become
acknowledged duties, even for children who might
have had little to do with family. For those who have

for personal reflection

When you return home for visits, what are your reasons for going?

stayed in close touch, when family crises arise interaction multiplies. In the course of these returnings, issues that were held at bay during weekend or yearly visits come raging to the fore as siblings must work together and tasks of great intensity and intimacy lay bare deep feelings from childhood.

To Find Help in Times of Trouble

Some adults who left home in great conflict eventually return like the Prodigal Son in times of trouble to the place where, as Robert Frost reminds us, they have to take you in. The battles resume. But this time, some of them end, and others are cut short without a victor because all the combatants acknowledge the victory is not worth the battle. And relationships resume.

To Sort through Issues

Some adult children return home seeking answers to their emotional pain. Many people arrive at my counseling office because of a pain that won't go away with a simple aspirin or an exercise plan or an increase in the favorite denial system. One bright, happily married woman came because of occasional but terrifying panic attacks. Another man was disturbed at his own angry attitude that came out in every relationship. Another woman was agonizing over news of her husband's affair. They presented totally different symptoms. But a key to understanding them all lies in understanding family emotional patterns that have gotten stuck. I send each of them home, to current families and families of origin, to deal with the issues that have built up in their lives.

The panic attacks were the final bursting open of the Pandora's box of childhood horrors that had been neatly tucked away and seemingly escaped. The man's anger stemmed from unresolved anger at his father for needing so much caretaking. The husband's affair was related in part to the wife's emtional and physical distance learned from her parents. Each involved family patterns that had trickled down into current relationships and needed unearthing for healthy forward progress.

You may not have such dramatic pains at the moment. But perhaps there are irritations that don't go away, fears that issues will explode, concerns that you know will only grow larger if you do not do some exploring and changing now. If they are related to the issues simmering within your family, they are best addressed now. When the red light on my car dashboard goes on, my car usually is still running. I would like to ignore it or hit the dashboard so it will go off. But if I ignore it, sometime later I will find myself stopped on the side of the road with my engine smoking. So, too, with family issues that brew in the heart engine of relationships. When you see a red light of repeating conflicts, pre- or postholiday depression, or simply unfulfilled hopes, open the hood and start working. When you go home and tackle family issues, you may keep them from tackling you later on.

To Make the Most of the Family You've Got

A final reason for going home, for working on family relationships, is to make them the best they can be. In 1992, two days after she gave birth to her first daughter, my twin sister was told she had cancer. I immediately told my husband that our children were his for the time being. I left and went to be with my sister. She needed somebody to rock her baby, buy her clothes the right size and style, clean her bathrooms, massage her feet, and to be—just to be—with her. The crisis confirmed our relationship and what family meant to us. My parents prided themselves on having raised self-sufficient, competent adults. We had dutifully gone our own ways, loving our independence but knowing we would be there for family in a crisis.

After my sister's cancer, I wondered what we had fought the cancer so hard to secure. I realized we were not enjoying our relationships in the everyday good times. I decided not to wait for times when I was needed or even for holidays to visit. I determined to cultivate my relationships with my family in the best of times, despite our living far apart. My sister and I instituted a yearly spring birthday day together. We enjoyed it so much, we added a fall retreat day. And then last year, we twins invited our older sister to make it a three sisters' weekend, with no children or husbands. We enjoyed one another so much that it became the first annual sisters' weekend.

You may have a family that enjoys vacations together but can't seem to plan them. You may have a family that cannot get along but a sister you love to see or a father you admire or a mother you enjoy traveling with. Your family may be difficult to get along with but doing so may be crucial to your own maturing. This ensures that you will not find yourself in the midst of a crisis or a funeral regretting you did not make more of the people God gave you to learn from, enjoy, and love.

The Feel of Family Visits: Base Camp or Prison Grounds?

All of us return to family sooner or later, often or rarely. Yet the feel of these visits can vary greatly from family to family. For those whose families are indeed their warm launching pads of great love, family visits become a time for emotional restocking like hikers returning to base camp. For those who were glad to grow up and finally have a way out of the pain of family, this becomes a time of torturous returning like parolees to their prison grounds for a weekend. For most of us, the reality lies somewhere in between, often with a combination of feelings of both base camp and prison.

For everyone, it can be a labored repeating year after year of the best and worst of our family life, or it can evolve into a time for deep relationship work and growth. This book challenges you to make it the latter.

Home for the Holidays:
The Best and Worst of Times

Holidays are a natural time to see family. Not only advertisers but our poets and our own deep longings fill us with expectations at holiday times. We tend to assume that other families are having the sort of good time that we never seem to have. Other families are the Norman Rockwell and Walton families of America or even the happy poor we may have seen in paintings. The cheerful smiles and replies of "Fine" when we ask how others' holidays went lead us to believe that they do not experience the internal agony and grief that we do. On top of societal expectations, we place our own personal family expectations. These may come from past memories of good times that may or may not be repeated this time. They may come from encouraging family members who want us to make the effort to come home, their warm wishes in phone calls or letters. Or the expectations may simply be hopes that things will be different this time. Even when we do not have good experiences of home, we have high hopes for it.

For work at relationship growth, holidays are the best and worst times. They are best because, by virtue of their repeating rituals, they are easy to predict. At a holiday workshop, when I ask participants to tell me about their families, they will say, "My family is impossible" or "I can't understand them at all." Yet when I then ask them to tell me exactly what will happen when they are met at the door or as they gather to eat Thanksgiving dinner or disperse at the end of an evening, they without hesitation begin telling me exact, detailed scenarios that repeat visit after visit, year after year. This predictability of holidays gives one great opportunity to plan for changes.

Holidays are also the worst times for change because they are so laden with years of tradition and rigid expectations. The impetus to do things the same way pulls like gravity. The resistance to change can make it as difficult as pushing a great boulder up a hillside. However, that also means that even small changes at holidays can have dramatic effects. A step that seems small can be a great leap forward because it is so clear and has broken with tradition. And a change in a holiday is a sort of sacred change, for it feeds the deep heart yearning for celebration of better relationships at holidays.

Preparation and Disappointment

Lots of preparation, expense, and effort go into our family visits, especially at holidays. Television and store ads besiege us with their suggestions for the perfect material gifts for every occasion. They lead us to believe the myth that if only we buy the right gift, wear the right fragrance, spend enough money, serve the best foods, and decorate elaborately enough we will have a grand family time. Even men who leave much of this preparation to their wives still often foot the bills, hear about the hassles, and spend hours waiting in airport lines or traffic jams.

Often in my own returning from a trip to family and in my discussions with others of their trips, there are disappointments, sometimes agonizingly deep disappointments. Unlike the preparations, which are almost entirely of the material nature, the disappointments are almost invariably about relationships: the repeating fight with Dad over politics, the tension between sisters because of competition, miserable feelings from Mom's criticism about weight and looks, the inability to agree about what to eat for dinner or what movie to see. During family gatherings, intense and complex feelings boil within though the external façade remains intact: internal fury over a father's cutting jokes at which everyone laughs politely, deep self-doubt within the smiling dutiful daughter, knife-edge anxiety over trying to keep old rifts from breaking asunder around the holiday table. Even when the holiday is basically a good one, disappointment may arise in the question I forgot to ask and opportunities I missed simply for lack of thinking ahead about what I wanted to happen in my relationships.

People are easier to love at a distance. Family members are too well-known to ever be distant. We see their flaws and can detail their faults (as they can our own). Memories are happier without the dreary details of fights over who will ride in the car with whom, worry over whether the family drunk will make a fool of himself again, or boredom on the rainy day at the beach. Somehow time with people makes us all appear too human. In the refining fire of time together, the dross rises to the top of the pot quickly. And this is never more true than at holidays with all their intrinsic expectations and stresses. The repeating patterns of family tensions do not go away from absence and time. Like Old Faithful, they erupt with regularity forever, it seems. So we are once again disappointed.

A New Sort of Preparation

Going home requires a lot of preparation. Yet the most important preparation has nothing to do with gifts, food, decorations, or money. It has to do with what is most important: relationships. We dream of connecting and caring with the people we love (or are supposed to love) most in the world. Yet what we spend the most time doing to prepare for family visits involves things, often so many things that we have little time to reflect and prepare for the relationship challenges.

I've recently tried to do this kind of preparation at home. My typical process of preparing to have friends over for dinner used to include no thought for relationships. I would plan a menu, shop for groceries, and begin cleaning the house a day or several days in advance. On the day of the visit, my pace would gradually increase as I started mixing recipes, cutting vegetables, and tossing remaining clutter into closets or desk drawers. I usually am almost frantic during the last fifteen minutes, at which point I rush upstairs to change clothes while doing three last-minute kitchen tasks. By the time guests arrive, I am tired and just hoping the house is decent and the food edible. But I have given no thought to the purpose of our gathering as friends, much less to our typical relationship snags or goals for growing a deeper friendship. Yet at the end of the evening what will make me smile or sigh will not be the well-displayed entrée or the blueberry cobbler but the tone and substance of our interactions. My preparations have not been invested well.

I am trying now to do dinners differently by including relationships in my preparation. I am trying to consider or pray for the people who are visiting as I peel potatoes, not worrying so much whether the dish will be done on time as whether I've been alert to the hope of their coming. So, too, for family visits. I am trying to remember to think about the people and interactions and ways to move toward my relational hopes.

Homework

When couples come to me for couple's counseling, I find there is one factor that is by far the most critical one for determining whether their marriage will survive and grow or whether they will not make it. That is the degree to which they are both willing to work on the marriage. I have seen bright couples with boundless potential end their marriage because they were not willing to commit to working on the relationship. I have seen couples mired in hurts from generations past and current traumas overcome these to move to a deep, loving relationship. Regardless of their resources or my expertise, the most important question is, "Are you willing to work, really work, to build this marriage?" The same is true in regard to work with one's family of origin.

My husband has said on more than one occasion that he would love to learn how to wrap packages in a fancy, attractive way. Recently we were at an Asian bookstore and I saw a book on tying bows for packages. I grabbed the book enthusiastically to show him. He held it rather limply, looked it over, and put it back on the shelf.

> *for personal reflection*
>
> **How much work are you willing to put into your family visits?**

"Why aren't you getting it?" I asked.

"Well," he said, "I don't know if I really want to do it that much. It would take a lot of time and effort."

So he has not learned to wrap packages, neatly or elaborately, but he no longer speaks longingly of finding a book, for he considered the cost and decided against it. If you are dreading the next family visit or telling stories of the last one, you now have an opportunity to either work on learning a new skill or give up your complaining. How much work are you willing to put into your family visits?

Hope

When I told my sister about the topic of this book, she asked, "Do you really think a book can make a difference?" She's honest in her skepticism. In fact, many people spend years in therapy with only gradual success in this endeavor. However, I write this with some hope, based on several experiences. The first is my own life and the difference in my own family visits as I have tried out these principles. When I enter holidays blindly, I almost always return feeling sideswiped or even run over. When I began to put in even small amounts of relational planning, I reaped a harvest—sometimes small and occasionally gigantic.

A second experience that gave me hope was a short workshop I gave, inviting participants to plan and prepare for relationships over their holiday visits. I asked the participants to consider a few straightforward questions:

- How would you describe typical interactions at home during your visits?
- What part of this would you most like to change, insofar as it involves you?
- What is one very small, doable step you could take toward this change during your next visit?
- What reactions do you expect and how will you respond to them?

We discussed their answers, worked on ideas, and planned together. After just two sessions focused on these key questions, participants reported some remarkable changes. I was surprised, as were they, by what effect their specific, careful planning of one small change made in the family scenario and their own sense of hope. A few people returned telling stories of resistance and upset by others in the family worse than we had predicted. The most common experience was that changing one's own behavior significantly altered the feared scene with positive results. And occasionally everyone in the family expressed having experienced the same problems but not knowing what to do or not having the courage to make changes.

Home-Going, Not Homecoming

Key to the relationship preparation and the hope for growth is our approaching our family visits as a home-going more than a homecoming. Homecoming brings to our minds the idea of a child finally making it home and collapsing into family arms, bed, and routine. Occasionally, when we are unusually ill or have completed an exhausting task or just need to be totally off duty, home may be just the place for this respite. But when we are grown-ups, this cannot be our primary approach to family visits.

Home-going becomes more of a pilgrimage to find and become ourselves within the soil of our home relationships. Long-term family growth will occur only when we shift from childlike homecoming to an adult stance of home-going: prepared and willing to work rather than to collapse relationally. That work involves discovering the walls in the relationships, choosing our destinations, and taking initiative for the sorts of visits we wish to create. Rather than returning to the nest to be cared for as children, we must journey as adults to join our brothers, sisters, parents, and other relatives in the joint task of building family relationships.

Yellow Bricks for the Road

Even on grand journeys, we start by walking single steps, usually starting with the closest, most manageable ones. In The Wizard of Oz, *Dorothy was told to follow the yellow brick road to reach the Emerald City. So, too, there are practical, helpful steps that become our home-going "yellow bricks." Those steps are to know the roads not to take, become a family observer, sort trash and treasure, rewrite just your part, learn from walls and discoveries, and dig deeper to gratitude and forgiveness. These practical pointers are the first steps toward the larger work of changing old, unhelpful family roles and becoming your full adult self.*

Chapter 2

Avoid Dead-End Roads

obert Frost spoke of the difference between taking the easy road and the road less traveled. On a journey, there often appear ways that look easy or short but turn out to be dead-ends or swamps. Since you may still be trying those familiar routes that I have seen fail time and again, let me begin with a warning about which roads not to take.

Road #1: Not Going Home

When family pain is greatest, the easiest route seems to be not to go home. If there is always a fight at Thanksgiving, one way to take care of that is to not be there. If your family is too smothering, you can handle that by just going in the opposite direction. A man once said to me with great pride, "I'm free from my family problems. I left home and I've never gone back. I cut them off completely." Unfortunately, he did not realize that staying cut off is as intense a relationship to family as being totally dependent. Huge amounts of internal emotional energy are required to avoid someone—going out of your way to stay away, preparing how to handle the enemy if you meet them unawares, warding off any inner longings for home. A cutoff, in relational terms, is often simply the flip side of smothering control, the mirror opposite of overinvolvement. And we carry our patterns into other relationships. This man not only had no relationship with his family of origin, he had also been divorced twice. I think there was a connection.

I remember a woman in New York who came to see me. She had gone to great lengths to get away from a controlling and critical mother; in fact, she had taken a job in Africa, thinking this would be far enough away. Unfortunately, while she was there she developed severe migraine headaches that eventually forced her back to the States for medical attention. She was sent to me by a doctor who found nothing medically wrong. As we explored her tensions, we discovered that her efforts to avoid her mother were causing intense internal stress. She had to do the hard work, with great support, of facing her mother in Chicago. She had to deal openly with the anger she felt, find ways to express it without running away or having headaches, and address her mother directly.

> *for personal reflection*
> _____
> **What dead-end roads have you tried in your family?**

Besides taking too much emotional energy, family cutoffs also keep us from dealing with our pain and learning ways of handling conflict that will lead us toward better relationships. When we cut ourselves off from family, we develop a relational pattern of dealing with conflict by saying, "If the going gets rough, I just get going." While it is healthy to learn to say no to painful abuse, simply running from our whole family situation keeps us from learning to face our wounds and building healthy relationships where possible. Good relationships of great intimacy never develop without dealing openly with differences.

In rare situations, when there is clearly ongoing abuse, a cutoff is the recommended approach and in fact is a healthy step toward growth. In truly toxic, evil situations, the best thing is to set clear boundaries and move forward with safety and freedom. However, for most families, complete cutoff is a reactive, angry response rather than a healthy differentiating initiative.

Usually those who choose to cut off must sooner or later come to terms with their family. All too often this happens only at a time of crisis, frequently at the time of a critical illness or death. I know an oldest daughter who in her late twenties cut off her parents whom she felt were too controlling and critical of her. Not until twenty-five years later, as her father was on his deathbed, did she reconnect. She managed to reconcile not only with her father, who died shortly thereafter, but also her mother with whom she now has an enjoyable adult friendship. Yet she is sad for the years lost during her own children's growing up—their loss of grandparents, her loss of parental help. Many people are nudged to go ahead and address their family issues by the recognition that they do not want to do this work in the hospital intensive-care room or at the funeral home, when the bitterness of siblings and spouses can often never be undone. Working ahead of time with the living is a lot easier than dealing with guilt and grief after a parent or sibling dies. At some point we have to grow up, face the tough adult tasks, and make some peace with the most powerful people in our lives.

Road #2: Going with the Flow

The most natural approach to family visits is simply to go along with the way things have always been. We close our eyes and let the natural flow of family rules, traditions, fights, and flights take over. We float like a log on the river, carried along by the current. We may try to "lay low" to avoid conflict or be a good daughter to try to make everyone happy. Secretly we hope that things will get better, that time will heal or mature us all. We hope against hope that things will somehow miraculously improve, saying to ourselves, "Maybe this year will be different."

My experience has shown that families tend to repeat their patterns with tremendous predictability, and those who go with the flow will find the same flow year after year. The current is particularly sure and strong at holidays because it has flowed the same way for so long. A friend recently was discussing the upcoming Christmas dinner with her mother, who was telling her that everyone had better be sitting down for dinner by 5:30. She suggested that her mother tell people an earlier time if she was determined for dinner to begin at 5:30 sharp. Her mother asked why and she replied, "Well, Mother, just because every year for the past twenty-seven years, someone has been late." Families are predictable, even if what is predictable is chaos. If you wish for growth and change in your family relationships, going with the flow will not get you there.

Road #3: Trying Just a Little Harder

Sometimes we determine to try harder with our families, thinking that in the past we have not done a good enough job and that things will turn out if we just try harder. We give lots of effort but use the same basic approach we have always used, thus magnifying or intensifying the problem.

So if you are the person in the family who takes care of everyone and everything, then you may try with each family gathering to do a better and better job of planning, baking, buying, preparing, and taking care of all that needs to be done. You imagine that if only you get everything right, Dad won't drink or your brother won't blow up or your sister will appreciate you or whatever. The problem is that the drink or the anger or the lack of care from other family members has nothing to do with you. No matter how hard you try, you cannot keep a person with a drinking problem from drinking or a person with an anger issue from exploding or a person who resents you for your birth order from resenting you.

If you are the family peacemaker, you may think that if only you can catch things earlier, use a little more humor, or handle things more assertively, the visit will work out okay. You go determined to have harmonious family interactions and ready to take any put-downs, sarcastic comments, or even abuse so as to keep the peace and allow for a harmonious family holiday. It is possible to keep the lid on things, but as the emotional pressure mounts your clamping the lid on tighter does not make things truly peaceful but only temporarily calm—like walking a tightrope is calm.

Generally, just playing your role more intensely does not alter what bothers you most and never works to change others. Trying some new approaches, even if the steps are small, may yield more substantial hope for family progress.

Road #4: Being the Expert to Change Others

Although this book is about relationship change, there is an important caveat: We do not have the power to change anyone else. When I talk about making family visits better and when I ask people what one change they would like to make, the first answer usually has to do with changing someone else. "If only my mother would not smother me." "If I could just get my father to not yell so much." "I'd like to stop my brother from ignoring people and keep my cousin from talk-ing politics." Neither you nor I can change other peo-ple. I cannot help you keep Peter from blowing up, calm Martha down from her anxious preparations, stop Jane from buying so much, or get Billy to do something to help others. The only person we have much possibility in changing is ourselves.

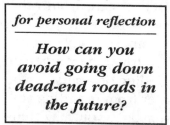

for personal reflection

How can you avoid going down dead-end roads in the future?

Another way we can ensure failure is to become the expert on what is wrong in the family, what could be better, or how everyone could grow in the direction we wish. If we put ourselves in the role of master choreographer for a whole new family dance, we are likely to be giving commands to thin air. This invariably will be resented by everyone else, since they know us to be "just" the little sister or the bossy brother or the controlling father. Hope is realized not when you plan changes for everyone else but when you begin taking small steps toward change for yourself.

Road #5: Expecting Total Change

The strategies suggested here, even if we follow carefully every yellow brick in the road, will not alter the basic makeup of our families. We may think we've been born into the wrong family or wish we might exchange ours for the one down the street. Unfortunately we cannot (and they cannot exchange us either). The families we were born into are ours for good and, since we cannot change them, we must be content with the changes we can make in ourselves. Often people I have counseled fairly successfully will return several years later with a problem that feels like the ones from before. They will be terribly distressed, wondering if they have made any progress at all. Even when we grow, our core issues that arise under new stresses remain the same. We will have to keep plugging away at depressive tendencies or quick tempers or difficulties speaking up. So, too, with families. If your family tends to erupt into huge fights, you may learn to leave before the tension gets too high or plan quieter times with individual members. But the tense tenor of family reunions is likely to always be the same. If your family wants everyone to do everything together, you may learn to take some time out for yourself. But the natural suction toward togetherness most likely will be there forever. So do not aim for a family personality change or a total overhaul.

Aim instead for minor adjustments, small steps in the right direction. Better to try tiny steps that move you in the right direction than large steps that leave you hopeless about progress and stuck in the old patterns forever. If your family always has huge political discussions that erupt into major fights, don't expect to end up with a family that talks politely about the weather and the Bible. Instead, be happy if you can simply leave for a walk in the fresh air before you burst into tears. If your family never talks about real difficulties, don't expect to suddenly confront Dad's alcoholism. Instead, perhaps you can talk about some minor but real problem of your own and what you are doing about it.

What We Can Do

Once you have recognized these major dead-end roads and your tendency to drive down them, you are ready to put your energy in a fruitful direction. Keep two principles in mind as we now move to the practical steps in this section. First, always think in terms of your part, what you can do, and how you wish to change. Second, keep your steps small and manageable.

This may seem quite limiting. But think of the family scenario as a dance that has followed set steps for years. Consider what happens in a dance when one person changes the steps, even in a small way. The whole dance in some way is altered. The set pattern can no longer go on. The whole system must shift. You cannot entirely predict it, nor can you control others, but you can change your steps and you can trust that in some way that will alter the dance.

Remember, too, that when you are able to make even small changes in what has seemed an unchangeable situation, it can seem like a dramatic transformation. When you have experienced the weight of family chaos for years and are able to add one piece of personal order, you feel like a conqueror. When you have experienced the inevitable fights year after year and manage to leave before the final bloody round or step aside to dodge blows meant for you, you are a true champion. When you have experienced family love that never quite gets expressed and you are able to perform a demonstrative gesture, you become the sage.

And even when you cannot change others or significantly alter family dance steps, you can grow personally. You can grow by facing your fears, honestly coming to terms with the realities of your family, and developing an independent sense of yourself. So do your part, take small steps, keep walking patiently, and one day you will find all the yellow bricks one by one have led you to the Emerald City—and beyond.

Chapter 3

Step Back and Become a Family Observer

*I*n order to go home and stay grown up, we must first address the natural family "suction" that tends to draw us back into old childhood feelings and roles once we cross our parents' threshold. The first brick on the road home is one that helps us maintain our adult size: learning to shift from reactive participant to active observer.

Shifting Perspective

Imagine yourself entering your family with new glasses or a new role. Instead of your usual role, you need a shift in perspective from reactor to observer. This crucial change will allow you to see what is going on, your own typical role in it, and what you want to change. As long as you are simply reacting to others' behavior and expectations, you are powerless to make changes. So the goal is to emotionally step back in order to gain perspective and be able to view with more objectivity not only your family members but also yourself. Some of this shift occurs naturally during adolescence when we begin to notice what is wrong with our parents and to differentiate ourselves from them. At that stage, we do it primarily through open rebellion, silent subversion, or unconscious acting out (which some people continue!). When we leave home to go to college, live on our own, or get married, the process usually speeds up if only because we are exposed to an environment different from our own family.

I remember vividly one of my first experiences of this shift from participant to observer as a freshman in college. In order to communicate more naturally and save money on phone bills between Virginia and Boston, my parents and I decided to send audio tapes to one another. This plan only lasted for about two tapes; nevertheless, it was enough for me to have the shocking experience of listening to my mother on tape and realizing for the first time that she had a deep Southern accent. Only after hearing people with lots of different accents could I hear her voice objectively. I was shocked by the sound of my mother's voice. It had always sounded normal. From the perspective of Boston, it sounded Southern. Distance can help you see, or hear, your family in perspective.

Ask Your Mate or Friend for a Description of Your Family

> *for personal reflection*
>
> *Get an outsider's perspective on your family.*

Having a roommate or getting married gives you an observing perspective. Growing up, we assume that all families operate the way our family does (or else like some TV family). Then we move out, live with a roommate, or get married and we find out from close exposure that family rules, roles, and expectations differ greatly. Likewise, others begin to see your family and comment. Your mate or friend sees your family as an outsider, someone who is not a natural player and does not know the rules. Asked, and even unasked, your spouse can tell you a great deal about the dynamics of your family.

Imagine Watching a Video of Your Family

To help you change perspective, imagine yourself watching a video of your family. Watch the interactions, the gestures, the motions. Listen to the voices, to who is speaking in what tone, and how others react. Try to consciously move from being an actor or actress into an observer or even a critic of your family drama. If you were to write

for personal reflection

If you were to make a video of your family history, which would be the most memorable scenes?

and direct a movie of your family, what would it look like? Exaggerate some of the personalities and features to make your internal feel of the family clear.

Describe Your Family to a First-Time Visitor

Perhaps you have invited a roommate or friend to meet your family. Maybe you even gave him or her some clues about what to expect so as not to be surprised or unsure of how to react. If you were asked for a thorough briefing on your family before someone new met them, how would you describe them? Who are the people and their personalities, their typical attitudes and actions, their interactions, the overall atmosphere of the household? If you are comfortable writing, consider writing out the highlights of your family description and drama. This will help you get an observer's perspective on them.

Consider Family Atmosphere, Rules, and Roles
Use questions to help you in observing. Consider the overall atmosphere of your family. What word or words would you use to describe your family? Warm, friendly, chaotic, vibrant, playful, serious, sad, silly, intense, fake? Perhaps it helps to think of other families so as to describe your family by way of contrast.

Next, try to list your family rules. They are not posted on the front door or even scribbled on a piece of paper held by a banana magnet on the refrigerator door. Nor are there relationship pattern manuals for families like flight pattern manuals for pilots. But every family has certain inherent rules that govern family members. Sometimes they are spoken, loudly and frequently. But much of the time they are unspoken rules about emotion and relationships that you pick up like a language simply from living together. We know them from the words and reactions we learned around the dinner table (or TV), coming and going over the years, growing up with our parents. Rules range from "peace at any price" to "always speak up for yourself," from "don't make Mom upset" to "let baby sister have whatever she wants," from "pretend to have a good time" to "always complain about something." What were the spoken or unspoken rules in your family growing up?

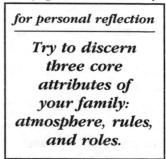

for personal reflection

Try to discern three core attributes of your family: atmosphere, rules, and roles.

Finally, think about the different roles that family members play. Hero, martyr, clown, peacemaker, financier, boss, doll, informer, organizer, philosopher? Particularly pay attention to your own role. How do you enter the family? What is your job in the family? How do you react to different situations? These questions reveal your role.

Examine Strengths and Weaknesses

Now consider, as a movie critic might a fine production, what works well and what does not. What are the strengths of this family? Sometimes the strengths are obvious: a warmth and connection that keeps people caring no matter what, humor and love of life that makes each day full of energy, flexibility to take whatever comes, or sense of independence that makes individuals able to stand on their own. Sometimes I meet people who think their families are totally worthless. Yet as we talk, almost invariably there are strengths. Sometimes it is simply the strength of having survived with so little that gives people an incredible fortitude as well as gratitude for the smallest blessings later on. Sometimes it is a strength of personality that, although it brought harsh abuse within the family, yielded in its children a determination to contribute positively. Always our parents have given us gifts for which we can be grateful, even if only the gift of life or the learning that comes from tough situations.

Next consider the weaknesses in your family. For some people, these spring forward with intensity as the things you have hated, complained about, endured, or fled for years: alcoholism, raging anger, smothering control, or depression. For other people, the weaknesses are discovered in the subtleties that resurface after spending a lot of time with each other. Some people think their families are perfect families, the model for what family life is supposed to be. In these cases, thinking about weaknesses can be hard or can feel like a betrayal. Often, even where alcohol or abuse is present, the family view of itself is wonderful, which makes coming to terms with the problems even more difficult. However, over time difficulties mount and eventually erupt in one way or another. Of course, our spouses can be particularly helpful when we get stuck in assessing our family's weaknesses. They usually have had to wrestle with the weaknesses all too personally as they deal with what we have come to take for granted. Spouses or roommates are almost always able to see with more objectivity and can help us, especially if we believe we come from a model family (and family members who may find no one good enough for their perfect child).

Whether you feel that your family tips more heavily on the side of strengths or weaknesses, every family has some of each and moving into an observer role can help you put them in perspective. Often the family's strengths can feed into its weaknesses or vice versa. Families come in incredibly different varieties, and it is vital that you learn to see your family with adult eyes if you want to work toward growth.

Different Types of Families

Let me describe a few different kinds of families I have known to help you begin to consider your own family.

The Togetherness Family
Some families are particularly warm, caring, and close. Togetherness is the most important value about this family. Doing things together or talking together, sticking up for each other, and trying to

agree on things are family hallmarks. People may finish each other's sentences, two or more talk at one time, stop by without calling, open doors without knocking, and baby one another with care. Families exist to be there with and for each other as much as possible.

If togetherness is a top value on normal days, holidays become the pinnacle of this family's closeness. Especially if they have become spread out from each other geographically, holidays are a time to reaffirm the closeness of the family. So everyone must be there, in one place, preferably in one room with as much contact as possible for as much time together as possible. Not coming for a holiday gathering or not being present for the special family traditions is a terrible affront in this family.

While caring and connection is the great strength of this family, it can become a trap as well. The trap happens when closeness is valued at the expense of natural independence and sameness is championed to the denial of individuality and diversity. Togetherness becomes a trap when it be-

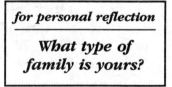

for personal reflection

What type of family is yours?

gins to feel smothering rather than nurturing, dependent rather than empowering.[1] The goal of the adult child going home to this family can be to affirm family care while creating some boundaries and limits to closeness that smothers.

The Family from Chaos City

Often as I listen to someone's story of their recent family visits, I hear the words, "You'll never believe what happened!" And yet if I ask these people about their past visits or even about an anticipated visit, they describe with almost clockwork regularity the bursting forth of some disruptive scene. One never knows just what will happen in these families except that surely something unexpected can be expected. This is part of a family atmosphere of flexibility, individuality, and at times, chaos.

These families are made up of members who are different from each other, go their own way, disagree with each other, and meet back at home mainly to refuel, release, or collapse. Yet on some level, they wish that perhaps at least for a day or two they could be like some storybook or TV ideal. Holiday upsets are common when this is your family because you realize your family is so unlike the perfect television family. Rather than being brief respites in the separateness of the family, visits can magnify the chaos with so many people together, little idea of how to keep peace, and few skills in the area of positive communication.

The strength of families like this is the independence that they cultivate in their members. People learn to take care of themselves and to be ready to deal with all sorts of surprise situations. However, they are weak in the togetherness that Hallmark leads us to believe family gatherings should demonstrate. Consensus, peacemaking, and togetherness are rarely achieved, or if so not for long. The goal of going home, then, can be to keep some small routines for yourself, express some warmth, and be prepared for the unexpected.

The Family of Disciplined Days
A tight sense of family order is the overriding theme for some families. Roles are clear, often with the father as a strong authority figure. Everyone knows how they are expected to behave and what the rules are . . . and most people follow them. Outsiders

sense that this is a nice, well-behaved, perfect family. But underneath this family's external functioning, there often lurks a subtle fear—fear of the consequences of breaking a rule, fear of upsetting the matriarch or patriarch, fear of a sudden outbreak of anger.

Family visits in these well-disciplined families are prepared carefully according to standard traditions and expected routines. Yet the normal stress of a family visit and added busyness of preparations increase the likelihood of a blow-up and thus the underlying fear. Often the priority of tradition robs the visit of any spontaneity and fun. The goal becomes following the rules as carefully as possible to keep the sense of order and avoid the anger of the disciplinarian. Tiptoeing or walking the straight line can become the attitude of the day, with warmth and flexibility sadly missing.

Families like this have the strengths of order and predictability. One knows just what to expect and what is expected of them. The weakness is the lack of flexibility and warmth. Breaking out of the mold is tough, and speaking your own mind is hard to do. The goal as adults is learning to set and follow some of your own rules as well as allowing more spontaneity in your life.

> *for personal reflection*
> ___
> *How would you describe your family to a stranger?*

The Down in the Dumps Family

For some families, life is particularly difficult. Often due to real tragedies or hardships but sometimes due more to a depressed outlook on life, these families lack energy and hope. They do the best they can to get by, but even daily tasks seem overwhelming.

They hear and fear all the bad news on TV. They expect the worst and sometimes receive it. These families survive and often there is great strength in just that. But when entering these families, one is left with an overall sense of isolation and depression.

Visits hold little hope for these families. In fact, they probably make less effort to prepare for visits and expect less than others do. They've accepted the fact that life is not a bed of roses and have given up trying to cultivate one. They just want to get through and go on without too much fuss.

The biggest strength in this sort of family is simply that they have survived, often through real difficulties. Somehow, they have kept going and have given at least physical life to their members. The weakness is, of course, the pervasive pessimism and depression that keeps hope from arising and saps energy from everyone. Individuals from these families must learn to reach out to find other resources to bloom and grow and then bring some of this positive life with them as they re-enter the family. If you are able to find life outside the family and bring it with you, family visits can actually become a bright spot for those with little hope.

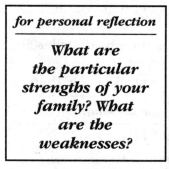

for personal reflection

What are the particular strengths of your family? What are the weaknesses?

Can you begin to identify your family in one of the descriptions above (or a combination of them)? Can you begin to spell out the unique rules, roles, and atmosphere of your own family as you take on an observer perspective? What stands out most clearly? What subtle but definite messages come through?

Learn Stories Back a Generation

Once you have begun to observe your family, it is helpful to consider finding out the stories that have gone into the making of the rules and atmosphere in your family. Almost always there is a story, a history, a reason behind the making of a family rule. Yet often we do not know those stories well and only live with the outcome of them.

There's a funny story about a family that cherished the recipe for great-grandmother's ham. This recipe involved taking one large ham, cutting it in two, adding raisins, brown sugar, rum, and cinnamon, and then baking. A great-grandchild once asked her mother why the ham was cut in two. Not knowing the answer, she asked her mother, and her mother asked her mother until they learned that great-grandmother's oven was not big enough for the full ham! The recipe had been handed down with instructions for the ham to be cut in two. Although needed several generations back, this part of the recipe was no longer required with modern ovens. Emotionally, we may have needed certain aspects of a family recipe to survive or prosper several generations back but may not need to keep following them in new generations. Only by going back and learning the stories can we understand the emotional recipes and what we want to be sure to keep and what we can discard.

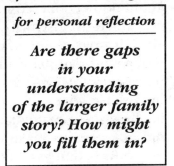

for personal reflection

Are there gaps in your understanding of the larger family story? How might you fill them in?

Sometimes the stories we learn are dramatic. One woman who had always sensed her mother's anger, especially toward her father, discovered while doing some courthouse research that her father had actually been charged with rape of her mother. The charges had been dropped and the couple married, but this discovery gave her a whole new understanding of her mother's anger as well as the stamina of them both continuing in the marriage and their commitment to her as their child.

A very bright architect I once saw due to her plaguing depression made incredibly slow progress. She had realized that her mother probably struggled with depression though her mother always tried to handle things on her own, stoically. A turning point came in her work when she found out a long-hidden piece of her mother's history. Apparently her grandmother had been Catholic and had married a Jewish man, for which her whole family cut her off. A few years later, with a three-year-old daughter, her grandmother suffered the loss of her husband, who was killed in Auschwitz. When the architect discovered this piece of the family story, the depth of her mother's grief and loneliness—which had been passed on to her—suddenly made sense. And her own sense of unspoken, unnamed depression was finally given a reality and a history. The realization did not instantly make things better, but it allowed her to feel compassion toward her mother and take up her own work with more focus on the real grief work involved.

Other times the stories that are turning points for us are little ones that suddenly give us great insight into our parents. My mother once told me about her mother's controlling everything she wore and making everything for her, seemingly all out of corduroy, to the point that we joked about whether she had had to wear homemade corduroy underwear. Hearing those stories, I began to understand why my mother did not have a very strong sense of herself and appreciated in a new way the heroic effort my mother made to allow us to have choices, especially about what we wore.

In learning the story of your parent, it is important to realize that the qualities and behavior of the person you know as a grandparent may be quite different in style or intensity from that same person as a parent twenty years earlier. I remember vividly a conversation with my mother as we were leaving my grandmother after a visit later in her life. My grandmother had become rather senile, and my mother was easily irritated with her. I said something about not getting so upset because certainly my grandmother had been there for her when she was able. My mother slowly shook her head in the negative, and I suddenly realized she had never gotten from her mother what she was now having to give—patience, care, understanding, gentle acceptance. She had gotten

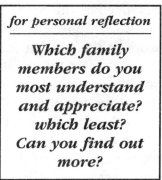

for personal reflection

Which family members do you most understand and appreciate? which least? Can you find out more?

a lot from her mother. But she had not gotten from her mother what I had gotten from that same person as a grandmother—unconditional love and care, cheer, and comfort. Even if a person is fairly similar as parent and grandparent, what is fun and exciting in small visits can be overwhelming when you must live with them as a parent.

Learning the stories behind the rules and the emotions of your family does not take away your own experience or pain of living with them, but it can give understanding, which in turn can lessen your reactive anger and bitterness. You may begin to take your parents' actions less personally as you see them in a larger context.

This involves asking questions about the family history, on a visit home or even a phone call, to learn more about your family, especially those people and events that have not been talked about. Imagine yourself to be a journalist researching a story or trying to understand a culture. If you had to give a description of your grandparents and family life with them, what would you not understand? What are you curious to know more about? Who would be the best person to talk to about the gaps in the family history, and what questions might you ask them that would begin the storytelling? You want to gain a larger perspective, fill in the gaps of understanding, learn stories that give color to the black-and-white framework of the generations past.

Think particularly about the parent with whom you have the stronger reactions. Now imagine what questions you might ask to discover more about that parent's experience with his or her parents, stories of growing up that might help you understand how that parent learned the patterns of relating that affect you so strongly. The tone for these discussions cannot be one of a nosy detective or police officer looking to assign blame but more like a curious child eager to hear a story or an explorer interested in learning about a new place. Here's one such simple question: "I've never heard much about what your father was like growing up. Could you tell me a few stories?" This can open up many parents as historians and storytellers for their children. Or you can focus a little more specifically with questions like these:

"I know it's important to you that we learn to

solve our own problems. What about your own growing up made you decide that was so important?"

"You work so hard at the family's all being together. What about your own family as a child taught you that value?"

"You always said we didn't know what hard work and tough times were like. Can you tell me about some of those times that make you understand it?"

It's better to start with nonthreatening questions that your parent is likely to want to answer rather than zeroing in on the toughest areas first.

Remember that if you have not heard these stories before there may be a good reason why. It may simply be that your parent is so oriented to the present that he or she has not told you much about the past. But there also may be secrets or family land mines that your mom or dad does not want you to unearth. This should not keep you from initial exploration but be prepared to observe how discussions are thwarted and what questions are avoided.

If the parent with whom you have the more intense relationship seems too difficult to approach initially, you may want to start by asking questions of others with whom you can more easily relate. Not only do they give a different perspective on the same story, but they may also be able to tell you more facts without all the emotional reactivity of the person directly involved. An aunt or uncle may be able to give you a perspective on your parent's childhood that you never fully understood. Cousins may have heard stories from their parents that your own mother and father never told.

This first step of simply standing back to observe

and learn is helpful not only because it is an easy way to begin for you but it is also an easy way for others.[2] It is much better to become interested and eager to listen than to risk jumping in too quickly with suggestions or dramatic changes. Remember, you've been in your family for all of your life and will be for the rest of your life, so this journey can be done yellow brick by yellow brick over time.

Chapter 4

Sort Treasure from Trash

*L*ike the photographer who moves from the wide-angle lens to the zoom, the next yellow brick on the road to better home-going involves looking at the specific scenarios of your next family visit. The perspective is still as an observer rather than an actor in the drama. But you must now look carefully at the particular scenes that will be played out.

Family scenes can usually be predicted because we have been in them so often. The actors remain constant with the same personalities, reactions, and typical moves even though the dates and times change. At holidays, they are especially predictable because the nature of holidays is to follow set traditions or routines (even if the tradition is to do something different or the routine is to have a chaotic gathering with at least one blowup between varying members). The family script has been rehearsed many times and is just sitting on the shelf waiting to be taken down and the parts played one more time. There may be a few changes here and there to make it up-to-date, but the core of the script remains the same.

Our tendency is to make a brief general review of the coming holiday, the sort we might make as we pack the last bag and wrap the last present. We might remember holidays as warriors remember long-past battle scenes or as alumni remember college days before going to a reunion. We tend to remember the glory, the good memories, the sweeping scenes. Yet when we get closer, going to a new war or the actual reunion, the details of more complex and often more negative emotions spring forward to catch us by surprise. Only in returning to the scene are we gripped by fear when we come across a certain smell that was associated with a particular battle or by loneliness as we walk old halls that we once entered for the first time away from family.

Have you ever noticed how, when packing for a trip, it is difficult to imagine weather other than what one is experiencing in the present? Once when packing for a December trip to New York from my home in Houston, I actually forgot my winter coat. I rarely used it in Houston. The weather was 80 degrees outside. Not until I got off the plane in wintry New York did I realize my mistake. Since then, I have been careful when I pack to try to visualize myself in the place I am going and imagine what it will be like so that my clothes fit not only the weather but also the activities I will be encountering. So, too, emotionally and relationally we need to plan and imagine ahead of time so that we are not caught without our relational coats in wintry weather but are ready for the interactions that we will endure.

Review the Specific Family Script

Now when you plan a visit home, rather than simply entering the stage as the actor playing the oft rehearsed part, take time beforehand to review the script. Return in your mind to past visits, taking the role of a movie critic. Sit back and review the old scenes from your past visits, using them to help you predict what will happen in the upcoming visit and make changes in your part of the script. Or imagine you are on a basketball team and you are getting ready to play a team you've played before. You have the tape of the last game to examine the moves of the other players, look at your own strengths and bad moves, and decide what it is you most want to work on improving for the next game.

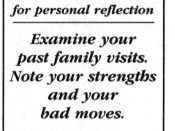

for personal reflection

Examine your past family visits. Note your strengths and your bad moves.

In your mind, push the automatic play button and let the tape roll. See yourself arriving, greeting your parents (and siblings, cousins, grandparents, children, etc.), beginning to interact, continuing with the typical family activities and attitudes. Work yourself through the hours or days you expect to be there and imagine the likely scenarios, allowing yourself to be an observer but taking into account your reactions, what you like and dislike.

Ask yourself questions to help you consider specific details of what the holiday will be like. Who will arrive when and in what mood? How will interactions begin? Who will initiate and in what way? How will others react? How will the conversations or actions progress? What will the tense points be and how will they be dealt with? What will the open conflicts be? What will be the hidden frustrations? What are some specific scenarios you can predict? How will the visit end?

Once you've reviewed the script for a typical family visit and your picture of family interaction is clear, begin some inner sorting.

Sort Trash and Treasure

A store on the Westheimer antique row in Houston is called Trash and Treasure. To someone who walks in, at first, it seems to be just a junk shop, full of things that should have been tossed in the trash long ago. But if you look carefully, there are treasures that are precious antiques or unique items that would be a great find for just the right home. Some of the items that might be junk to one person are a treasure to another, and vice versa.

When a parent dies, children gather to go through the personal effects. A sorting occurs of what is no longer of value that we are ready to toss and what is precious for the memories and love it rekindles in us. I would suggest that such a sorting is valuable long before anyone dies, and not primarily sorting of things we own but of actions, attitudes, and traditions that families pass on.

Getting Started

First, what is it about your family interaction and this particular visit or holiday that you treasure most? What aspects do you love that restore or energize your soul and relationships? What do you want to be sure to keep or even expand during this family visit?

> *for personal reflection*
>
> *Which parts of your family visits do you cherish?*

Treasures in my family include the gathering of the younger generation to play touch football, the canoe trip down the river with Dad, a lunch alone with Mom, sitting on the top of the mountain ridge at sunset and sunrise. Treasures I know from other families include Mother's welcome-home hug at the door, the hot debate on issues of public concern around the dinner table, family tamale making in the crowded kitchen, smelling and eating Dad's cinnamon buns, having a picnic after a long day in the sunshine, sitting out on the back porch or on the fire escape listening to the sounds of the city. Taking time to determine these precious parts to your family visit is the first step to being sure they continue and grow.

Second, what is it about your family interaction and this visit in particular that bothers you the most? What is it you want to be sure does not happen so far as it depends on you? What is the event or interaction or attitude that leaves you feeling upset, frustrated, or depressed? If there were one thing, perhaps one little thing that would improve your visit, what would it be?

For example, as I considered a summer visit home, I realized that what I treasured most was a quiet half-hour on the top of the hill at my grandparents' farm watching the sunset and the next morning the sunrise. What I disliked most was the time spent worrying and talking about all the details of food and bedding. Reviewing another typical visit, that of our yearly Thanksgiving visit to Virginia to be with my parents and cousins, I realized that what I liked most was all the young cousins playing together and a few meaningful conversations one-on-one with a family member. What I disliked most was being stuck inside for three days, talking and eating without ever getting outside (though the men did by going deer hunting). In other families, the difficult spots have included the argument that invariably erupts between a daughter and mother that ends personal sharing, a son's feeling trapped inside the house listening to his mother's woes without being able to go out on his own as an adult, a woman's feeling responsible to be the maid when she enters her mother's home.

This careful examination is the crucial prerequisite to making a positive change. You must know what you wish most to keep about your family visits and what you wish most to change. Thinking about what you love most, consider what you can do to maintain or build on it.

for personal reflection

Which aspects of your family visits do you enjoy the least?

Considering what you most dislike, think about what aspect of this might be open to change, remembering that you can only change your part in the scenario.

Plan to Develop the Treasures

Realizing what you treasure most, consider how to be sure that it is included as part of your visit. Let others know how much you value these particular aspects of family visits and be creative about ways to make the most of them. For example, once I realized how much I loved time on the hill at sunset, I made it a point to stop other activities and go specifically for sunset watching whenever I am in Virginia. After I found that the best visits with my father were when we were driving alone somewhere, I tried to ask to go with him on one of the legs of our minitrips during a visit. When I discovered a good way to have fun with my mother was at lunch out, we began scheduling these regularly, especially if the visit was likely to be hectic otherwise.

Just as we sometimes store our treasures in special

boxes to preserve them, our family relationship treasures can be maintained better if we turn them into established traditions. A spontaneous trip to the beach with my husband and children and my older sisters was so enjoyable that we have set it as a regular summer occurrence. By doing so, it gets on the calendar, and over the years all of the relationships in the two families have deepened by having a regular time we love together. The little traditions of a sand-crab-catching contest, a sunrise walk with my niece, and ice cream bets over the NBA playoffs add to the fun and fill our storehouse of memories. My love of sunset watching will soon become a tradition maintained by a hilltop garden that invites a regular ritual of sunset (and moonrise) watching by all the family.

Treasures developed in other families I know include evenings for intellectual debate around a fire, cookie baking with grandmother and grandchildren on Saturday mornings, walks on the beach to work out conflicts, mother-son singing performances, and long chats between grandson

for personal reflection

In what ways can you keep or enhance the relational treasures on your next visit home?

and grandmother. Whatever your treasures are, be they large or small, hard to arrange or hard to avoid, be sure to make the most of them and make them happen as much as you can.

Choose Specific Trash to Change or Discard

Because our family scene seems so daunting, we often fail to tackle even little changes. Yet this is exactly how we must begin, by focusing on only one or two specific scenes for change on any given visit to make a relatively small and manageable step. Think specifically of one thing you would like to see different on this next visit with family.

You might choose a small but repeating interaction pattern. One woman told me of sitting by passively as her mother tossed into conversations critical comments about her son's long hair and non-traditional job. A son described his father's conversation about all his physical ailments that dominate family discussions while everyone else gradually stops talking and leaves one by one. One young woman was annoyed by the way her mother would repeatedly ask her each morning what she wanted for breakfast even though she had repeatedly asked to be left alone and given time to wake up.

Or you may want to focus on a major problem scene:

- Your brother picking on your sister to the point of her bursting into tears while you watch helplessly

- Your father getting drunk and telling off-color jokes to which you react angrily while your mother pretends everything is okay

- The filling of time together with activities to make sure there are no quiet opportunities to talk about any real problems

- The dinner conversation that starts with everyone talking until your uncle ends up on his political diatribe, at which point everyone leaves one by one

Whether you decide to work on a small repeating pattern or a specific, upsetting scene, consider the smallest details so you are prepared for the likely scenario as well as possible. Imagine particular places and moods and conversations and interactions.

Trash and Treasure in a Single Scene

Often you may find that what you love and hate most converge in a single family scene. This requires careful sorting to be sure to keep the gems of the family visit while changing what spoils the fun. One woman's family had a tradition since she was small (begun by her grandmother or maybe great-grandmother) of making tamales together every Christmas Eve. The family would gather for tamale making in the evening, followed by going to the midnight Christmas Eve service. Returning home, they would all eat the tamales and open their presents. However, she and her brothers and sisters each had several children, and when everyone gathered and opened presents it went on so long into the wee hours of the morning that she ended up overwhelmed and exhausted rather than encouraged.

I asked her to identify the treasure and the trash of that tradition as she was anticipating an upcoming Christmas. She said that making the tamales together was great fun and something she would hate to give up. But coming back after Mass for everyone to open presents became chaotic. The treasure was the long-held tradition, with its history, its gathering of family to work and to eat together on this sacred evening. The trash was the enormity of the gift giving and late hour with many children. With some work, she was able to maintain the tamales and Mass with the family while bowing out of the late gift giving. Most traditions in families, like this one, need to be reconsidered from time to time to hold fast to the treasured part while shucking off what no longer works.

Look at Your Part

Once you begin reviewing the family scene as it has been played out before, and you imagine it repeating, you will need to focus in on your part. Since you must give up efforts to change others and remake your family, the focus must be on the part you play in the scene; that is all you actually have the possibility of changing.

For example, although you despise your father's getting drunk, you must focus on your part in the scenario that you can change. Your part may be continuing to stay at a family party after your father is drunk and the conversation has degenerated, or it may be getting into arguments with your mother about stopping him, or it may be going along with everyone in ignoring what is happening. Your part is the crucial part in the change process because that is what you are responsible for and all you can work on personally.

One woman noticed how she became passively helpless as her mother began her critical review of her children. Another man realized he made small but indirect, cynical, and ineffective attempts to interrupt his father's hypochondriacal conversations. Another woman recognized just when and how her anger button would get pushed so that she exploded out of control. Yet another man began to see his part in following the family mode of filling time with activities so that there was no time for personal conversation.

Your focus has narrowed to a specific scene in a typical visit home and your part in that scene. You are ready to begin creatively considering small steps toward change.

Chapter 5

Rewrite Just Your Part

For well over a year, Rosie had in therapy faithfully tackled the emotional issues of sexual abuse, sibling rivalry, and anger at her mother. One day she came into my office with a new sense about her. Having clearly come to a watershed moment, she sat down and declared to me, "I have listened to and told my family story for a long time now and you know what? I think I'm ready to start writing." It was time for her to have a say, to take charge and make changes for herself, to not just react to the past but start living into the present. So, too, you have come to the place in the book where you need to start writing. You are ready to consider how you will change your old routines and rewrite family scenarios to better fit your own hopes for family visits.

Acting Differently

You have considered the specific pattern or scene that you dislike and your role in it. Consider now various ways you could act differently. Be creative in thinking of options so as not to get stuck in the way you have always acted. Consider the ways in which you have moved out of your traditional roles in other aspects of your life. How would you respond in a similar situation on your job or with close friends or people you had just met? How have you matured in relationships apart from your family? Might you be able to bring those more adult, grown-up ways of being into your family? As you think creatively about the particular scenario in your next visit home in order to plan for a change, remember three things.

Rewrite Only Your Part

You first stepped back to observe and listen to what has been played over and over. Having a good picture of the scene, you must now move from script reader to script writer. You have one crucial limitation in your writing assignment. In this homework, you are only allowed to rewrite one part, your own. You must leave the parts of your other family members as written, knowing quite clearly what they are. Find creative ways to change just your part.

You cannot eliminate your father's temper. You can, however, determine to speak up rather than tiptoe around him, leave a harsh conversation rather than endure his tirades, or address his outbursts maturely so that he is the one left looking foolish. You will not be able to change your family to become warm and accepting to your partner, whom they dislike. But you might be able to speak a word of support for your partner when they begin complaining or voice your difficulty in feeling torn between

> **for personal reflection**
>
> **Creatively consider new ways of acting in the old scene.**

the people you love. You cannot give your mother the confidence she has never had, but you can work to accept her for who she is and enjoy her gifts rather than encouraging her to do things she will always fear.

Make It Manageable

With the understanding that once you rewrite your part you will also have to play it, consider one other guideline in your writing: make the script changes small and manageable. Don't set yourself up for failure. Make tiny changes that can be easily adapted to the previously memorized script. If you are the tired heroine chef for the family, give up fixing a huge breakfast every day, but continue your cooking gift to the family. If you become a meek turtle in family discussions, do not plan to present your thesis on life but aim to contribute one or two statements that come from your heart. If you revert to being the family clown, do not give up humor for the family visit. Instead just try to hold your tongue a few times when you can sense it is a distraction. If you are the family martyr and scapegoat who endures the anger of others so as not to set off World War III, don't plan a final battle strategy. Just plan to speak up for yourself calmly but firmly a few times.

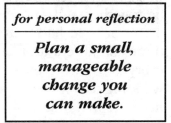

for personal reflection

Plan a small, manageable change you can make.

Of course, once you arrive with family, you may find that what you thought was a small step feels like a mammoth task, in which case you make it smaller still, until it feels manageable. Only you know just how big or small any step is emotionally.

Rewriting Is a Continuing Process

Unlike a play that may only be performed once, your family drama is a play in progress. Rewriting is best done in small increments that can be accomplished little by little like growing a tree to shift the direction of family movement. One wonderful thing about family relationships is that we almost always have plenty of opportunities, for we will see our families over and over giving us opportunities again and again to grow. There is no need to make huge changes all at once. Rather, we need to be slowly but surely moving toward health and growth. Choose one area, one scene, and one manageable part of that scene to begin making a shift. Think of something small that you really imagine you can do and begin with that step.

Hang onto the important vision that you are no longer just an actor but also a writer, and the play goes on and on. Our lives are a story in progress and our family history is always in the making.

My Own Rewrites

In my family growing up, people always tended to be together, unless they were sleeping. Even in the bathroom we had togetherness. Growing up with three daughters and one bath, we learned to use every area of the bathroom simultaneously. On my wedding day, we had a schedule up on the bathroom door to make sure everyone could be accommodated. Privacy and alone time were not things I grew up knowing or valuing. As an adult, one of the things I learned to treasure was quiet time, solitude in my days. Going home to visit my parents could, therefore, deplete my tank completely within a few days, until I learned to rewrite my part so as to keep personally fueled in the old home environment. At first, I would just take my time in my room after seeming to go to bed for sleep or in the morning before appearing as an awake person available for conversation. More recently, I took the bold adult step of actually announcing (as my husband had always felt free to do) that I was going out for a walk by myself. Counter to all the unspoken rules I had thought existed about always being with others or available to help, I selfishly carved out refueling time. But a funny thing happened on the way to my forum: By doing this I became a much more pleasant person to have around the rest of the time, and I found I could enjoy visits of greater length.

Another modus operandi in my family is for all members to be always present and free to interrupt each other anytime. Private conversations somehow never occur. Perhaps they are thought to exclude others. As an adult, I realized that what I value is personal, one-on-one conversations that can get close to the heart. Unlike others who feel safest as long as conversation is of the least common denominator variety, I feel bored and frustrated if I spend time without talking more personally. As I mentioned in chapter 4, I made several rewrites for myself to address this wish. First, I realized that as an adult I could actually ask my mother out for lunch, accomplishing several goals at once. By relieving her of lunch duties, I free her to be more relaxed and able to talk. And by our being apart from the kid and home hubbub, we actually have a chance for adult conversation. At first, besides the general enjoyment of going out, it was a bit awkward. But I managed gradually to have the courage to be an adult who was more honest and open with my mother, and she came to rather enjoy having one daughter to herself treating her to lunch for a change.

for personal reflection

By doing things that refueled me, I found I could enjoy visits of greater length.

Finding one-on-one time with my father has been a greater challenge, not only because he has no interest in eating out but also because he has little interest in staying still or talking in great depth. Nevertheless, I discovered that car trips, with seat belts holding us in place as we were moving toward another activity, were a place to talk. So I looked for times, short or long, where I could end up in the car alone with my dad for some portion of each visit to get in a private conversation.

After I had successfully rewritten these smaller parts in the family dramas, I tried a couple of larger rewrites. I must admit that I violated the rule to rewrite only my part. But I did this after I discovered that my family did not resist my initiatives but simply needed to know what I wanted rather than having to read my mind. My first major initiative came the year my husband and I hosted my family for Christmas in Houston. I began anticipating (and dreading) taking on the hostess role as my mother had defined it—captive to everyone's needs all the time. I decided I did not want to get to the end of the holiday exhausted and resentful at having played cook, dishwasher, and hostess. And I knew others did not want that either, as they had our good Fletcher blood in them making them always look for ways to help out. So, I decided to allow people time off from being helpful by suggesting they sign up in pairs to be "on duty" for specific meals and dishwashing. What this would accomplish for me was two things: first, everyone could be "off duty" a majority of the time; second, those working could have one-on-one time in their efforts together. When the first suggestion was met with cooperation, I added my second suggestion: that women be encouraged to go out for lunch together in pairs during the holiday, allowing something better than least-common-denominator, group-interruption conversations. That, too, to my delight has taken hold.

I tried another major rewrite several years ago at Thanksgiving. Thanksgiving had become a regular time to go back to my family in Virginia, with our pull revolving around the annual extended family Thanksgiving feast and (for the men in the family) deer hunt. My husband and sons grew to love this gathering of the clan and time out in the woods. Meanwhile, I enjoyed seeing their enjoyment, and I did rather like having a calm few days without three boys running wild around me. But I did not like staying inside with the women due to the danger of being out with hunters all around. Living in the city, I loved going to Virginia to be out in the country, yet as a woman I was confined to old-fashioned women's work or play. I determined to find a way to get out on that beautiful land myself at Thanksgiving and, ever looking for ways not to be outgrown by my sons, announced that I would begin deer hunting. The first year, I borrowed a gun, but by the next year my husband had bought a gun for me to legitimize my rewrite, and I have learned a whole new way of being in touch with nature through the quiet cool listening of the deer hunter in me.

Rewrites As Varied As Families

My rewrites have been particular to me and to my family. So your rewrites must suit yourself and your family. Every family has its own set of strengths and weaknesses that you alone understand fully (or at least know in your gut even if you don't understand them!). And you have your own brand of wishes and frustrations to guide you as an adult going home. Let me share with you a few of the creative ideas I have seen tried by adult home-goers from different types of families.

Space for Togetherness Types

When family togetherness, both physically and conversationally, is strong, any effort to set a boundary or stand on your own is helpful. One woman decided that during table conversations she would quite nicely but clearly state that she had a different perspective on a topic. Another man learned to thank his mother for her offer to straighten his closets but tell her he lived more flexibly and did not wish her to work at cleaning his place on her vacation. Another woman braced herself to respond directly to sarcastic comments by her brothers rather than letting them slide. A man whose mother relied too intimately on him decided to acknowledge his youth and suggest she talk to her new husband whenever she brought up things that he felt were inappropriate for him to hear. One woman decided to prepare a healthy salad for her own lunch rather than eat the normal family fare, a major step in her tightly knit family. One couple made a point of going out, just the two of them, during visits to their families of origin so as not to get swallowed up in the larger family. In a family that avoids discussion of problems at any cost, another couple worked hard to honestly answer the question, "How are you?" with at least one open sentence even if that was never pursued any farther.

> *for personal reflection*
>
> ***Setting one boundary in close families or enforcing one rule in chaotic families is a first step to progress.***

Order in Chaos City

Maintaining inner order and outer structure requires personal rewriting in families that tend toward the spontaneous, chaotic side. Several people I know have now planned to stay in places other than the family home if chaos reigns too rampant. Young adults may tell their families they will stay with a high school friend. Couples with children may decide to rent a hotel room. This gives them the ability to return to a place of stability if things become too wild, to maintain some routines for themselves, and take time for recentering. Parents of young children have determined to keep bedtime or story hour rituals even when visiting grandparents. One young woman rewrote her part to respond calmly to her sister's provocations instead of engaging in her usual hysterical reactions. Another woman prepared to speak up for herself or her children if her father in an inebriated state made a rude remark. A man invited his parents out to eat so that discussion would not get too heated and so that they could politely leave when the time was right. Taking control of phone calls was another woman's strategy, deciding that if her brother began talking or acting in certain ways she would tell him she must go and hang up the phone.

Life for the Downcast

Families that are known for their sense of discouragement and lack of energy require grown children to find ways to maintain their own sense of hope. One woman decided on Christmas day when things were getting a bit dull in the afternoon that she would plan to go ice skating whether or not anyone else wanted to join her. Another woman decided to

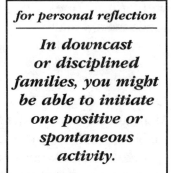

for personal reflection

In downcast or disciplined families, you might be able to initiate one positive or spontaneous activity.

stay only part of New Year's Eve with her parents and to go to a more cheery friend's home after that. One man prepared to initiate more conversation about his own activities rather than simply allowing his parents' ill health to consume the conversation. Another man took responsibility for launching a modest family activity that got his parents out for something fun. Even one step in a typical conversation or one different activity can help reverse the downward slide.

Spontaneity amid Discipline

In families of great discipline, adults going home have to bring an extra portion of warmth and mercy to add to the family pot. One woman whose mother is devoted but not nurturing decided she would add a hug to her greeting of her parents. Another woman learned, when her mother began criticizing her son for not following a traditional career path, to express her own appreciation of her son's creativity and courage in trying to pursue what he really enjoyed in life. A man decided to share some of his feelings of hurt and sadness with his father, with whom he had always had to be tough. In rigid families, simply deciding to break a small family rule, to do things the way you do in your own adult life rather than revert to the rule of your parents, can soften the atmosphere.

From Hamburger and Toothpaste to Heart and Soul

When I work with married couples, we will often spend a great deal of time on whatever the particular argument or upset was that week. Often the focus is some seemingly silly thing like whether the toothpaste cap is replaced or who got the hamburger out of the refrigerator to defrost. Sometimes people will say that it is ridiculous to argue about such a little thing or spend time and money in counseling about the hamburger (or the way the trash was collected or not having an umbrella in the car or the tone of voice ordering drinks at McDonald's). The reason we do is not because any one of these everyday activities is so important but because each little activity is repeated hundreds or thousands of times in the course of a relationship, and the pattern between people over the toothpaste or hamburger is indicative of the pattern throughout the relationship. Like a dance instructor taking time to go over a small series of steps slowly and carefully to correct the mistakes and learn smoother ways of dancing together, we look at the small incidents to identify larger issues. By changing a simple but repeating behavior that reflects a much larger attitude or way of dealing with others, we begin to make significant headway. Life is lived full of the small, everyday interactions. By making a tiny change there we can begin to address the heart and soul of our relationships.

The same goes for any visit home to see your family of origin. Pick one simple behavior to restructure. It may be in an area that gives you the greatest feeling of refreshment so you can be sure to keep alive and growing during your visit. It may be a small but certain step toward change of one of the destructive dance steps you have identified in your family. Perhaps you will make a modest effort both to grasp hold of life and change what you dislike. By choosing a manageable step and taking responsibility for your part in it, you may avoid the feeling of hopeless shrinking, gain a sense of adult empowerment, and take personal responsibility for building better family relationships. You may become an instrument of life and hope within your family. Like a worm that loosens the soil and quietly breaks the hard clods to keep the earth fertile, even small quiet movement enriches the ground of your family life. In this way you counter the tendency to personally shrink and learn to become more consistent as an adult wherever you are.

As you address the most basic issues through even the simplest rewrite, you are no longer a victim, a child, hopeless and stuck, but have become an active participant, an adult, hopeful and growing. By addressing your part in family patterns, actively though humbly, you will not only avoid shrinking, you may actually grow taller.

Chapter 6

Be Prepared for Walls and Discoveries

In my thirties, I made a clear effort to move toward being more of an adult with my mother. She had for so many years given of herself and taken care of us on all our visits home. I thought it was time for her to get something back from all her parenting efforts since she did, after all, have three rather competent adult daughters. So I invited her to go with me to a destination of her choice for a weekend away together. She chose New Orleans. On that trip, I made a wonderful discovery and encountered a powerful wall.

I arranged for flights and a bed and breakfast, and we met for a weekend of fun. We toured the aquarium, delighted in beignets and coffee at Café du Monde, and had our picture taken as two smiling adult women before boarding a cruise down the Mississippi. In the process of that trip, I made a wonderful discovery about my mother. I met a woman who could relax and enjoy new adventures without worry. I had never known this part of her, and I suddenly realized it was because I had never known her in any setting other than one of great stress. After all, I had been born a twin to a mother with a fifteen-month-old. All my life with her, she had had children depending on her, needing food and clothes and care and mending and rides to ball games and money for college. Even after we had grown up, I primarily saw her on trips home as a mother hosting the hoards. This trip was probably the first time I had ever been with my mother in a setting in which she was not a mother on duty but rather a woman on vacation. We were in a setting for me to begin getting to know her as a person—and perhaps allow her to finally enjoy her daughter as another woman on a journey and not a child to be cared for.

One of the things I had hoped for in this relaxed and personal setting was to talk about some of the painful times in our family that had occurred while I was too small to remember. I figured dinner on Saturday might be good for a more serious, open discussion. Yet as I prepared in my own mind to ask her about this time, I found my stomach in knots, my hands clammy, and my voice as uncertain as anyone I have ever spoken to in my office. I am a psychotherapist, which means that every day I ask people to tell me about their most troubling and sensitive issues, and for the most part they speak and I listen. I am trained to know how to help people tell their stories and break through walls to face their pain. Yet I became immobilized, turning suddenly into the scared child afraid to broach a forbidden topic as I tried to execute a change in my own family.

Finally, I got up the courage to ask her about this difficult time. Her response confirmed my own wall as I realized I had broached one of hers. The resistance, both mine to ask and hers to talk, was palpable and powerful. I realized the wall of not talking about tough topics in our family was not a figment of my imagination but a clear command. She at first said she remembered very little, as the time was mainly a blur. A few halting follow-up questions by me yielded a fairly quick close to a touchy topic, though not without revealing a crucial story for my understanding of how much she gave in mothering three tiny children.

Our planned rewrites and changes for our family trips never go just as planned. They are only the starting place, and we must expect to meet walls of resistance and discover new stories along the way.

Walls: Prepare for Resistance

As you prepare to execute rewrites, be ready for resistance. If change were easy, it would have happened before now.

Fortified Walls

There was a reason why I had never talked to my mother about this difficult time in our lives and a reason why I had butterflies in my stomach. Somehow in the past I had gotten the very real message that we did not talk about this, and it was only confirmed that evening over shrimp in New Orleans.

I know a thirty-five-year-old daughter who finally gathered the strength to speak up to her mother about the subtle criticisms and disapproval she felt growing up. She found out why she had never done it before. Her mother got mad, refused to accept any responsibility, stopped talking to her, and over the course of a year would not even begin an adult dialogue. Although extremely painful and disappointing, this became a turning point as well. This woman came to realize that her mother would never be able to give approval or to hear criticism of herself. So she began to build a life for herself, buy a house, take a new job, and develop relationships with men, all of which previously had been put on hold waiting for her parents' approval.

Another person was the middle child of three brothers. Easygoing and successful, he had become the scapegoat of a younger sister's anger because he had not been the protective and responsive big brother she had wanted. At some point in most family gatherings, he would become the one to dump on, and his traditional role was to take the pummeling. He decided to speak up, not so much against his sister but in his own self-defense. This changed his helplessness in family gatherings, but he found that he had to give up the expectation for a mature, relaxed relationship with his sister due to her continuing deep-seated anger about many things.

Sometimes the resistance is massive, like a stone wall. Often such walls have been built through strong experiences unknown to you. Like a hiker on a long path built to go around a rock in the way up a mountain, you wonder why you have to take such a long way around. You may not have been told the story of a much earlier hiker who was killed slipping on the rock. Or you may know the story but may not have lived emotionally through the gruesome experience that gives such power to the family rule. So, a son who is annoyed that his mother is fearful of his playing football in junior high and later of his mountain climbing trek, may need to remember or hear again the details of his uncle's football accident and the months she spent visiting the hospital ward wondering if he would ever walk again. The daughter who feels her mother never lets her out of her sight and never trusts her to do things on her own is living with the guilt and fear of the mother whose first daughter was killed crossing the street at age eight. The daughter who lives with an emotionally distant mother may never hear the stories of chaos and abuse that her mother experienced and how she has lived her life to keep her daughter from the same. Trauma walls are never removed entirely for the person who has them, though they can be gradually lowered. Understanding them does not remove the difficulty they bring but does help ease the frustration and judgment of those in the next generation who must still take the long path, at least when hiking with parents.

Families do not readily change any more than other institutions. "We've always done it this way" is a maxim that applies not only to the church where I first saw it hung but to most families. Even when they have outlived their usefulness, traditions die hard. Painful routines are nevertheless familiar, and we all will keep doing things simply to maintain the comfort that comes with familiarity. This family "homeostasis" (dynamic balance) is like the pendulum that will still return to center no matter how hard you hit it. Even if you get an initially positive response to your change, don't be surprised if everyone returns to old patterns the next time around. Long-term change usually takes long-term effort, even in small areas.

> *for personal reflection*
>
> **What walls might you encounter as you try to change family visits?**

Cardboard Walls

Occasionally, we find that the walls we thought were so massive are now more like cardboard and fall over easily if we just knock on them firmly. I discovered such a cardboard wall the year I had my whole family for Christmas in Houston. When I got up courage to suggest my plan for taking turns being on duty, I discovered that in fact they all felt the same way I did. They were delighted to have a plan so we all could have some time "off the hook" for relaxing by being more conscientious about our "on duty" time. Everyone felt the same way, but no one had thought of changing the way things had always been done. All it took was the initiative and a good idea, and it was welcomed as a cold drink after a hike in the heat. The resistance in this instance came later on in the form of going back to old ways unless someone took responsibility each holiday for dividing up chores.

When you prepare for a family visit with a change in the dance steps, think about the possible walls that you may run into. Who knows if it will be a massive stone wall or a cardboard prop waiting to be knocked over? Like knights prepared to slay dragons, if you prepare for the worst, you will not be so surprised and disappointed if you encounter a battle. And if the dragon turns out to be a puppy, you can sit back and enjoy your new discovery.

As you imagine your rewrite for a family visit, imagine as well the varieties of resistance that you will encounter. First, consider what might keep you from executing your planned rewrite. What will be the hardest part for you and how can you clear that away? What or who will make the planned step most difficult? What reactions might you expect (remember to think in terms of the typical family rules)? Even after change is begun, most families try to regain the old homeostasis when a change is introduced, so anticipate how that might happen in subtle and not so subtle ways in your family.

Second, think about how you can handle the responses and resistance that you may encounter. Like a baseball player who gets stuck on first base not knowing how to run the

for personal reflection

How can you prepare for the resistance you may encounter?

bases when the other batters follow, you do not want to find yourself stranded in the midst of the family visit without having prepared for the whole game. Imagine several possible scenarios and what you might do, in the best and worst cases. Have several options with several people. If you do this planning, you may find yourself more likely to go ahead with that first step, knowing you are more likely to get all the way home.

Discoveries: Expect New Learning

The goal of family growth is not simply to decide on your desired course and follow it. A major gift is the discoveries made along the way—discoveries of history behind the walls that bring understanding, discoveries of the cares and hopes of others in the family, discoveries of personalities never fully known while dancing the same old steps with no variation.

When I give families homework at the end of counseling sessions, I use it in two ways. Certainly I hope they will be able to simply do it and gain from the exercise. But I realize that just as helpful can be what I learn from how they do or do not follow the homework. I sometimes learn that I have over- or underestimated their abilities, I discover a hidden roadblock, or I realize their need for further coaching. So, too, as you approach a rewrite in your family, be open not only to executing your plan but learning about yourself and your family along the way.

I made such a discovery one day on a visit home to see my parents. Early that day I had said I was determined to see the sunset. While helping out with dinner, my eye was on the sun, and at one point I left the kitchen and wandered up the hill to check out the sun's position. The sun drew me over the crest of the hill and farther and farther down the meadow for the best view of its position in the north-western sky. By then, sunset was in full, rich array and I was a quarter of a mile from the family. The yellow was turning golden, and I knew that if I left to tell my family where I was I might miss what I had come to see. So, I sat down in the field of grass, wild flowers, and cow dung to watch the light show across the Shenandoah hills. The Creator made a special show that evening. Gold turned to pink which then spread like dye through the clouds; just as it seemed the light would fade, neon pink arose and was flung across the sky.

While I was enjoying this scene, I worried that my family would be looking for me or would be mad that I was not helping with dinner. I might even have missed dinner. I could hear in my head the faint echo of my mother's agitated voice, "Where's your father? I don't know why he disappears right at dinner time!" But I stayed for the full performance, and even for the credits at the end of the show as the sky faded to gray. I slowly walked back to my parents' home, refreshed but wondering what kind of reception I would have. My mother ran to me. She was anxious and worried, but not about the dinner. She said, "I was worried . . . worried that you might miss the sunset." I had imagined she might be upset about the meal. Instead, she had put aside her own occupation with dinner and was worried that I would miss what I had told her gave me great pleasure. My image of my mother changed in that instant. I realized that she was not just anxious about dinner and her own concerns. She was concerned at the heart level with my happiness.

Understanding

I remember going to a new church in New York to give a seminar. The facilitator seemed quite nice but a bit slow and slightly awkward to me. I silently discounted her and the group to some degree. Later I learned that her passion for family ministry and the volunteer work she was doing came from having barely survived a car accident in which she spent days in a coma and weeks in the hospital. Suddenly in my mind the slow, awkward woman became an incredible model of stamina and faith. Hearing her story made the difference. So, too, with our families.

One young man I talked with was angry at his father for not being more positive, helpful, and involved with him. Yet this man seemed always to be taking care of his parents, helping them out, and running errands for them, while being angry with them much of the time. As he rewrote his part in family visits to take on less of this work he resented, his anger lessened and he had more constructive conversations with his father. One such conversation led to his father telling stories of his grandfather who had always been afraid to leave his home and never made any effort at all to be helpful with his family— ten times worse than what the father was like with the son. Listening to his father's perspective, he realized that his father had actually made a lot of progress in the parenting arena, even though he might be far from where this son wanted him to be. Understanding can help us to see that at a certain point we must realize our parents usually have given us their best, even if we feel that best is not all that we would want. We must take the emotional ball and run with it.

> **for personal reflection**
>
> **Look for new discoveries about who your parents are and what their own families were like.**

Asking your parents about their own growing up and their own parents and grandparents can give you new respect and understanding. Your goals may still be similar but the blame disappears, and working together through the generations becomes more possible.

New Talents and Relationships

When you change the dance, sometimes you discover that others can change as well. They may know the tango even though you've all been only waltzing for years. I did not realize my mother could relax and have so much fun. But then I'd never invited her to a weekend away without being mother, cook, and maid on duty.

Once, after a difficult few months recuperating from major surgery, I found the courage to ask my older sister why she had not been more involved to help me. She looked surprised and said that, since I had always been so capable, she had not thought there was much she could do for me. I invited her to resume an older-sister role and help me all she could, particularly if I was down, even if I acted as if I could handle things just fine. I had to admit my needs to gain the wisdom and care she had to give.

One woman from an extremely close, successful family came to me concerned about the increasing tension that she felt—tension enough to cut with a knife. Her aging father's growing stress was apparent in his becoming more remote and easily angered, her brother had left the family business after a recent blowup, and she was feeling overwhelmed in her task of keeping family smiles and harmony intact. In every effort to speak to and include her father in the emotional work, she was rebuffed by a stone wall developed by his military training and years of effort to be the strong man of the family. However, she discovered in her brother a companion not only willing but eager to listen to her and talk about the emotional issues never before allowed openly on the family discussion table.

Another man who came to me for depression began to see that the family rule of never speaking was costing him too much. As he began speaking to his two sisters, he found that one had suffered from panic attacks and the other had had to work hard on her marriage. Privately they had all been working on family issues; by his speaking up, he gained siblings who began relating to each other with a whole new depth of honesty and care. As he kept knocking on the walls, one turned out to have a hidden door to new relationships.

The work of going home is an ongoing adventure. Careful relational preparation is needed along with courage to follow new plans. But as you go, expect to discover all sorts of walls and possibilities. Rewrites always must go back for edits or new plans when old ones are complete or completely failed. The hope is in creating relationships between family members that are fluid and growing rather than stale and stuck. All families are really people in the process of becoming, books being written in the course of lives. You may be one of the authors, but you will only discover the full story along the way as you live it.

Chapter 7

Dig Deeper:
Unveiling, Gratitude,
Forgiveness

*T*he pivotal scene for me in *The Wizard of Oz* comes when Dorothy and her companions, after difficult journeying over many yellow bricks and securing of the witch's broomstick, arrive back at the Emerald City. Again they are in the chamber of the mighty wizard. The little dog pulls back the curtain only to reveal that the mighty and powerful one who was supposed to hold the key to getting home was just a common man, and an old man at that. Shock, anger, and disappointment fill me every time I view this scene. In many ways, however, this same unveiling must happen in our journey home as adults to visit our parents.

As children, we expect, imagine, and need our parents to be mighty and powerful. By virtue of their name and role, they become our closest images of the power, protection, and care of God. Yet as we grow up we discover that they are only ordinary humans and old (at least to us) humans at that.

The first practical yellow brick in our road involved moving from reactive participant to observer of family interactions. This last yellow brick involves the larger, deeper change of perspective that must happen as we move from being children to adults with our parents.

Wizard Curtains Unveiled

All of us have various curtains made up of our image or up-front picture of our parents. To a small child, parents loom large, both physically and emotionally. In the book version of *Oz*, Dorothy thought Oz was a great head; some of us think our parents are all-wise and always right, until we realize they make mistakes. The Scarecrow thought Oz was a lovely Lady; some of us think our parents are the image of beauty and have things all put together as adults, until they crumble one day or gradually grow old, bent, and wrinkled. The Tin Woodsman thought Oz was a terrible beast; some of us think that our harsh or cruel parents are huge powerful beasts trying to destroy us. The Cowardly Lion thought Oz was a ball of fire; some of us find our parents unapproachable and unexplainable. Most of us experience intense emotions: disappointment or betrayal or relief, when the real person of our parents becomes revealed.

I had my own curtain-ripping experience one Saturday night in New Orleans. I had always viewed my mother as the one who should give all the nurture and care my sisters and I could possibly want. And I had a sense that I had not always gotten as much holding and care as I would have wished. But for that weekend with my mom, I was giving up some of my expectations of her and trying to return something to her by taking her to New Orleans. As we ate

our shrimp that night, I finally mustered the courage
to explore those times in my early days when I felt
neglected in my nurturing.

I asked her to tell me about what it was like having
a fifteen-month-old and then twin babies. She said
with a slight laugh, "Hard," and paused as if wondering if she should go on talking as an adult with her
daughter. But she did. She went on to tell me about
a memory of her being sick with the flu, sitting on
the floor having to feed us with one hand while she
took steps away to vomit. I had known it had been
hard but the word was given new meaning for me
that night. I suddenly realized that the mother whom
I had needed to be an all-nurturing wonder woman
had been in reality a twenty-five-year-old girl strug-
gling to feed her children even as she was having to
take care of herself for the first time in her life. I was
left with a disappointment in realizing that I had no
wizard for a mother. But, as a human, she gained
stature in my eyes. I found a deep appreciation and
gratitude springing from this new understanding of
just how much she had given. I had a hard time
enjoying the rest of my shrimp that night, but I
gained great nourishment
for my soul.

A different sort of unveiling happened one August
afternoon in Virginia with
my father. I was home from
college and had the task of
asking my father a few
questions as part of a self-evaluation. I remember
vividly his answer to only one of what must have
been a whole series of questions. He had offered
plenty of praise and support, but when I asked him,
"What do you see as my weaknesses?" he paused for

> *for personal reflection*
>
> **When and how
> have your parents
> been revealed as
> humans rather
> than wizards?**

a moment and said, "I really don't know of any." At that moment I realized that his ability to be an adult with me was limited, for only a father of an imagined angel daughter still sees a person as perfect. The very thing that made him such a great adoring dad made for limited adult conversation and relationship. Later, when I married and had children, my sympathy grew for my mother, who took care of all the practical details of the household. I realized the very thing that most endeared my father to me, his playfulness, might be a hard thing to live with in a marriage when children had to be fed, clothed, and cared for day after day. I began to see my father, the saint, as a human.

Shocking Unveilings

For some adult children, the veil revealing the wizard may be pulled back in a shocking way, as it was for Dorothy. This can be due to the early death of a parent or the exposure of a parent's unknown alcoholism or hidden affairs. Or we may in our discovery of the family story come upon a suddenly revealing piece of information. One man I knew in New York held his parents in great esteem, though he struggled with a difficulty in affectionate relationships. His parents had both been extremely competent and devoted parents, but they demonstrated almost no physical warmth or affection. His mother refused to ever talk about her own family growing up, but at one point as an adult he did a bit of research. Going back to the library in the hometown where his mother was married, he discovered with a great shock that the headline in the paper the day of his parents' wedding was that his grandmother had killed his great-uncle. The reality was far worse than anything he might have imagined. In that shocking discovery, he gained a profound under-standing of the reason for the concrete wall of his mother's emotional distance. Emotions had been out of control in her family and had destroyed rela-tionships. She had gone to lengths greater than any of her children could know to avoid letting emotions come out and hurt people. To provide a stable, secure home, she had worked hard to stifle her own emotions lest they explode like her mother's. The cold but competent parent turned for him that day into a traumatized child who, as a parent, had heroi-cally protected her own children. And he moved from judge to astounded fellow human who was empowered to move forward with his own tasks.

Gradual Unveilings

More often, the unveiling comes as a gradual reali-zation. Like learning a foreign language, we learn little by little, hardly realizing our progress. In learn-ing a new language, we will wake up one morning having dreamed in the new language. We may little by little begin to see our parents' limitations as we become older or our mate points them out to us or our parents begin to age. When we go out running with Dad, one day we are beating him, and then one day we begin trying not to beat him, as he had done with us when we were small. At the library, we begin helping our parents find the large-print books. We realize that the wizard is only a man our size and shrinking.

Purposeful Unveilings

As a therapist, I sometimes play the role of Toto, pulling back the curtain in the interests of growth. A thirty-year-old trembles as she thinks of seeing her mother for fear of her disapproving comments. I ask her how she would handle another person who treated her like that. It emboldens her to grow up with her mother and realize she does not have to keep her mother as master of her emotional universe.

I encourage a forty-year-old attorney who dreads his father's rage to realize that he is now taller than his father and able to speak up, walk out, or even ignore his father's ranting as one might a kid having a temper tantrum. He begins to see his father not so much as the powerful tyrant as an adult toddler.

I encourage the teen who still feels unable to talk about his struggles with his model Christian father to ask his father about his own escapades as a teen. He returns amazed to tell about his dad's drinking on the beach every weekend with friends and almost getting run over by a car once lying in such a stupor on the ground. Such realizations help children and parents begin to walk and talk on more level ground.

Necessity of Unveiling

The journey home to see our parents eventually involves our pulling back the false curtains and learning to see our parents as they are, face to face, adult to adult, family member to family member. If we do not, we return with fantasies that will never be realized. And we fail to ever make the relationships what they might actually become within their limited humanness. Unveiling the wizard expectations we have of our all too human family

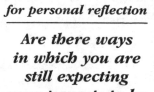

for personal reflection

Are there ways in which you are still expecting your parents to be all-powerful wizards?

(and ourselves) is crucial to planning realistic visits rather than magical ones that evaporate on contact.

Although the unveiling brings grief, fear, and confusion, it also frees us. It frees us to look to God alone for what we have sought from our parents. It frees us to journey alongside our parents. And it frees us to become fully our adult selves as the mantel of responsibility for our life journey rests clearly on our shoulders. For these reasons, we seek to promote the unveiling so that freedom may follow. That is the deeper heart work that arises in the process of becoming a family observer, seeking to learn the family stories, sorting through family interactions for our choice of trash and treasure, actively rewriting our part as adults, and opening our eyes for the walls and discoveries along the way.

Moving through Anger and Sadness to Compassion and Connection

In the process of the unveiling, a number of transformations or revelations occur in our relationship with our parents. No one progresses through them all in the same way: some of us skip a stage or two, and the degree of eventual connection varies greatly. But for all who do their homework, what starts off as difficult eventually becomes grounds for growth.

From Denial to Disappointment and Anger
Dorothy was at first furious at the wizard for making himself out to be something he was not. Because we wish so much for our parents to be all-loving and all-wise, when we realize they are not, we find ourselves terribly angry or disappointed. And when they have not only failed to meet our high expectations

but have actually done things that hurt us deeply, the rage and pain is most deep.

For everyone, beginning to acknowledge and to speak openly about what is happening in the heart of one's family begins the movement out of denial into progress. The speaking starts with an inner honesty that can be developed through journaling, letter writing, or prayer. But the voice needs at some point to have support and validation, so finding a trusted confidant is crucial as well. This may be a spouse, close friend, pastor, rabbi, or therapist but must be someone who will hear, validate, and support the process of family exploration and personal growth.

Once you begin to wade through the issues, you may find the water deeper than you had expected. Like a river given a new channel to flow in, the feelings and memories may keep coming. Your opinions, reactions, and feelings may gain strength as you provide a place to let them be heard. Whether the flow is a trickle or a giant stream, taking a short or extended time to explore, honesty in the anger and disappointments is necessary to growth and healing.

Sometimes confrontation with parents is needed, to clarify memories, to address wrongs, to reconcile hurts. Often forgiveness is eventually needed for true cleaning out of the hurt. And even that can be a long and sometimes ongoing process.

Not Taking Things Personally: From Disappointment to Sadness

Because we need them so personally and live with them so intimately, it is hard for us not to take the foibles and faults of our parents personally. Moreover, because children live with their parents, they oftentimes are the objects of their parents' anger or neglect. Children tend to assume that parents' anger or anxiety or depression or shyness or busyness has to do with them in some way: either it is their fault or at least they should somehow be able to make it better. We realize it is important to let children know that a divorce is not their fault but rather has to do with their parents' own difficulties. Likewise, it is important for children at some point to realize that their parents' pain is not usually their doing but comes from a source that began long before they were born.

For much of my life, I felt my mother's anger and anxiety—not directed at me—but ever present. I felt that I had better not push her too far. I think I imagined that if only I were a really good and a wonderful daughter, she would be happy. After all, she was a full-time mother; she gave her life for us. So maybe if I did really well, she would get good grades on her mothering and would be happy. So I was very good . . . very, very good. I got almost perfect school grades (only my twin sister got higher), won spelling bees and bird-house-making contests and track races. I did all the things to make a mother proud. And she *was* proud and very happy with me and with my sisters. But that did not take away her underlying worry and anger. Only fairly recently did I realize that this had nothing to do with me. Her children are probably what has given her most joy in her life (as well as plenty of gray hairs and full days). Her anger stems from years long ago before she even thought of children.

The movement from anger or disappointment to sadness is aided by stepping back to consider what your parent's life was like from his or her perspective. My understanding of my mother has expanded when I have taken time to think about the family from her point of view. I knew my grandfather as a vivacious, caring horse lover who presided over a food-laden table with stories of youthful adventures. However, as a young man he partied wildly, charged ahead with his own plans, and drank a lot. I can imagine my jovial grandfather as an insensitive father who inadvertently ran over his sensitive youngest daughter. My grandmother cooked fabulous food and let us run through her home and farm as children. As grandchildren we could shrug off her constant worries to an old person's perspective, but her daughter, who grew up with her, had that worrisome tendency almost genetically passed down to her. The same tremendous hospitality of my grandparents that caused us as grandchildren to feel always welcomed may have left my mother as a daughter feeling dragged along or neglected as her parents focused on social activities and community good.

A good student and obedient daughter who married a sensitive but fun-loving and somewhat irresponsible husband, my mother was the supremely good girl. But one can only be good and be run over for so long before the emotional toll becomes clear. Always doing what was right simply was too much for her by the time she had three infants within fifteen months. Her limits were surpassed and she collapsed into the care of others for a time.

As an adult trying to consider my mother's life from her perspective, my feelings of disappointment have turned to sadness. I have had to try to allow my mother to be herself, with her inherently worrisome nature and irritability, without being frustrated myself or trying to change her. My anger has turned in large part to sadness, for her own pains in growing up and for the anger and anxiety that have been her lifelong companions.

Identifying as Parents Together: From Sadness to Compassion

Recently neighbors of mine became grandparents when their son had a new baby. The grandfather, describing a conversation with his son who was bemoaning the difficulty of getting up in the night and caring for a colicky infant, laughed and said, "So the tables have turned now." His son is learning from the challenges of parenthood what his own father did for him. Another friend of mine has young adult children who have been unusually harsh in their judgment of him. But he knows they have not yet faced the trials of parenting teens or the never-easy challenge of stepparenting. So he says to his children, "Don't judge me till you're fifty."

I remember several times in my adulthood as I took on some adult task feeling still like a child: driving a car in Manhattan wondering how in the world I would survive, being a substitute teacher in my children's class and feeling more like a kid, going to a twentieth college reunion and realizing the likes of me run the world. Our parents were in adult roles, but that doesn't mean they felt and acted like adults all the time. I know a sixty-year-old who still feels like the shy child he was to a domineering parent and a seventy-year-old who still feels like the kid sister who could not kick the ball straight. Yet feeling like a child or not, we have to live as adults; as the popular song of a few years go reminds us, "We are the world, we are the people." Scary but true, for us and our parents.

When we become adults and realize how difficult the tasks of life are, we become fellow pilgrims with our parents in the task of living and loving. Often it is not until we have children that we gain a real appreciation of what our parents did for us. Our gratitude for the getting up at night and putting wet rags on our feverish foreheads grows. We gain wonder, realizing that they did this difficult parenting task without all the resources we have—maybe through the Depression or without a mate (or dishwashers or antibiotics) or with twice as many children.

Most people I know do give their very best to their children, even when that very best is not what their children most want or need. A man I know, who is described by his children as harsh, unavailable, and demanding, talks to me of how he lived his life determined to give his children what he did not have, laboring seven days a week all his life to be sure they had financial security: a home and college and cars. His wife also gave her very best: as a teacher and Christian, she devoted herself to being present with her family with love, affection, and faith. My own mother did not grow six hands or three laps to accommodate her task as mother of three infants, yet she gave all of herself to our care. We pull from the bottom and the best whatever we have in the basket of our lives to give to our children, though we all bring very different baskets to the task and have different ideas of what is the best.

From Compassion to Connection

I have thought I understood my mother in my head for a number of years. But an experience last year pierced my heart to move beyond compassion to connection. Like her, I have been a good girl, obedient daughter, and helpful, competent person all my life. I, too, had three children, though they were sons instead of daughters (which makes up for their being not so early or so close together I think). The third child was the one that tipped me over my sibilities. But not until he was five did I experience something like what my mother must have experienced of being totally out of control.

One evening I had had a full and trying day, counseling many people, carting children, and then getting a call from my husband that he would not be home as scheduled to relieve me to leave for a retreat I was giving. My inner temperature was close to boiling over when my sons got into a battle that reached the point of the elder starting to pour yogurt over the middle one in the living room. Why this particular evening and series of events cracked through my own resources more than all the previous challenges I will never know. But what I do know is that my adult self cracked into a million pieces for that moment as I dissolved into a raging child.

The next week, during a time of quiet, I was reviewing my early years and my mother's collapse when we were small. My own disintegration suddenly came to mind as I grasped in my gut the feeling of reaching my limits, going over the edge, and screaming out. I had not had an angry, drinking father nor three children by twenty-five nor financial stress on top of everything else as my mother had. I had had so many supports and good things given me that I had nothing to complain about. Yet I had reached the edge of my mental precipice and gone over just the last week, linking me to her across the miles and years. In my mind, we moved beyond mother and daughter to sisters. We were both women trying to do our best to take care of others and please others, having just too much to carry, losing it in anger, and being recipients of God's gracious mercy and compassion for our weakness and that of others. My home journey was coming full circle.

If we stay in the emotional position of an angry or disappointed child, we will never be able to move into the relationship that is possible with our parents as adults. If we do our own work to grow up, we may never have the ideal relationship but we will have a real relationship. I think of a driven, successful doctor. He was the product of a harsh father, who drove him despite his small size to be the starting quarterback on his football team. The intensity of his father's anger spilled over into the son's own marriage and family, forcing him to do his emotional homework. After acknowledging both his anger problem and his deep hurt from his father, he eventually was able to talk with his father, hear his father's story, and share his own wounds. The two began a relationship far surpassing any they had had before. Did it ever appear high in affection and mercy to an outsider? No. But compared to the place his father came from and he came from, there was a world of love.

> *for personal reflection*
>
> *Where are you on the journey from disappointment and anger to compassion and connection?*

How much connection will ever be possible between a child and parent ranges greatly. Parents cannot move farther with a child than they are able to move in their own emotional lives. A parent who never shares feelings honestly and openly is never going to be able to do that with a child, no matter how far the child progresses. Connection may be of a limited sort, with acceptance of that limit the hard work of this last stage. But without coming to terms with what will never happen, we cannot enjoy what can happen. Connection may mean simply watching a ball game together or going to a movie or maybe telling stories of growing up. But there can be a sense of companionship, acceptance, and appreciation that comes after moving through the harder stages of anger and sadness.

Gratitude and Forgiveness

At the heart level, two crucial disciplines make healing and connection possible. These are the deeper work regarding our treasures and trash. The first is gratitude and the second, forgiveness.

Gratitude

Without the sacrifice of our birth parents, we would not have our lives. They literally gave us life, physical life, even if we credit them with little more. I think of the birth mother of my adopted nephew and the tremendous gift of going through pregnancy—emotional and physical pain—all to give life to a child she would then give to others to love. I remember a pastor who provided great spiritual encouragement to his congregation. Only later did I learn that his mother was at an abortion clinic with $500 from the child's father when she turned around and walked out. I am grateful she did, despite all the pain she and he experienced in his difficult life growing up. Life itself is a huge gift that our parents have given.

Beyond that gift of life, the parents who raised us—biological or adoptive—gave to us in other ways. Even in emotionally abusive situations, there are sometimes redeeming qualities. I think of a man who felt tortured by the harshness of his father. Yet years later after his own wrestling with anger and depression, he sat with his father through the weeks of his dying. In those last days, he mustered the courage to speak with his father and to even thank him for what little positives he could remember. I was touched by his gracious reflection, "He was not an absent dad, and I am thankful."

Most of us have much, much more to be grateful for, though some have fuller cups than others. But think about your parents and what they gave to you. For the nights of getting up when you were little, the hours of watching your Little League games, the songs sung to you at night, and the prayers offered over your bed. For the "you can do it" look when you tripped during ballet or the skill learned by their insistence on your playing the piano. A list of what you are grateful for would be a good discipline for your homework.

Try to recall specific memories that capture the heart of what each of your parents gave you. I think of my mother sitting on a stool in front of the tall mirror in our hall, pinning up my cheerleader mini-skirt one round higher. For me, that epitomizes her faithful, devoted caring, not only in physical needs but with acceptance of me when my wishes were probably far from her own. I remember my father praying "Defend, O Lord, this Thy child, with Thy heavenly grace . . . ," the prayer that he must have offered softly hundreds of nights while embracing my head. Not a man of many words, those he spoke resonated deeply. I think of small-town Southern parents dropping me cheerfully in Harvard Square without showing me the frightened tears they shared on their way home. I am grateful for their encouraging me to choose and do and be whatever I wanted, without giving strong opinions.

You, too, must have those memories that capture the heart of your own gratitude to your parents. In the process of your delving more deeply into your family stories and working diligently at your relationship, bring their small and large gifts to the light for your eyes to gaze on with gratitude. Humans sacrificing for us, amazing parental giving even when it falls short of being godlike; in your own heart remember these to the givers them-

for personal reflection

Try to recall specific memories that capture the heart of what your parents gave you.

selves and to your Lord, the supreme gift Giver.

Forgiveness

Then there is forgiveness. Even the best of parents is not God and so does not have three hands or infinite patience or all-knowing compassion. We as children need so much love and care and no human can give it all. We acutely feel certain lacks and must eventually give them up to God, forgive our parents for the ways they let us down or failed to give all we would have needed or wanted. We must take the specific festering resentments and give them up— the resentment for not being home for us after school or for not knowing to listen closely the day we came home with a broken heart or for paying more attention to a handicapped sibling or for pushing us harder than we could take or for moving us away from our favorite street.

We must also forgive them for the more concrete wrongs. Even when parents think they are doing their best for a child, and especially when their own problems such as drinking or anger are significant, they can often hurt a child deeply. Some parents are just openly hurtful and wrong. If as a child you experienced deep real hurt, you may come to understand your parent's life story, but that does not eliminate your pain. What was inflicted upon you or the neglect you suffered does not disappear quickly or easily. The anger lingers and resurfaces even after you think you have stamped it down or dug it out. Yet you must address and deal with it lest it eat you up rather than them. And sometimes, when parents cannot change, the only resolution comes within our personal and spiritual wrestling with forgiveness lest we let the wounds grow wider or perpetuate the hurt ourselves.

Think here, too, of specific memories that symbolize perhaps patterns of a lifetime or multiple incidents of hurt. Look at them openly, speak the hurt clearly, and then when the time is right you may be ready to give them up on the altar of forgiveness. Such wrestling and giving up is often not a single incident but rather a process.[3]

> *for personal reflection*
>
> *Think about how you could work at letting go of your anger or resentment.*

Freedom after the Unveiling

Allowing parents to be human is a hard but freeing thing. It frees us from gnawing anger. It frees us to be grateful for the life they have given us. It frees us to add to our mothering and fathering through other friends and mentors we meet in our lives. It frees us to have a relationship with God, who alone can fill our deepest yearning for home.

My most memorable moment toward this freedom came one Mother's Day. I was kneeling silently in a full church, preparing for Communion and surrounded by the singing of the people of God led by the sweet voices of the children's choir. I felt embraced by the warmth and nurture of these people, this place, God's presence—held in the mother arms of God as it were. A gentle, sure, warm holding place of love was provided by the sights and sounds, smell and feel in that sanctuary. In my mind I saw my mother's giving all that she had of herself to give, feeding us even as she was sick, pouring out all the physical care of her energy to us. And the emotional calmness and holding that she could not give—because she had too many children and too few arms and too many worries—was supplied by all those in my life since, embodied this day within this pulsing body of love. She gave, others added, God filled. So on that day I saw the experience of my life. All the hands and hearts of mother, father, friends, and God made mother love complete that Mother's Day.

Finding Your Brain, Heart, or Courage

"So tell me about your family."

This relatively benign question, when asked in a serious conversation, yields a gamut of gut reactions. Some people continue the conversation easily, talking about their family almost like someone describing their garden, complete with thorns and special needs but with relative warmth and hope. Others tend to skirt the question, moving instead into talk of their own activities so that you will never get farther than the cover of their family book. Finally, a few people groan (inwardly or outwardly) as they realize you have hit a land mine. As in the children's game of Battleship, you have just hit their carrier, which is quite unsteady, and if you probe further it may sink.

Because of the great differences in families, the personal growth required in home-going work can take quite different forms. The practical steps of preparing for family visits lead us into the deeper, harder work of transformation. This involves changing basic, unhealthy roles within our families and growing personally despite our family's position. In this section, I will focus on three varieties of movement I have seen courageous people make as they have done their family work faithfully over time.

Those from basically nurturing, caring families must progress in the natural movement from child to adult. They must come to terms with their parents' natural limitations and take on more personal responsibility as adults. This is the natural but difficult process of growing up. In cases where children are particularly pampered, they must be the ones to take more initiative if growing up is to happen.

Sometimes families have children who are put in roles or take on roles too big for a child. These hero children parent their younger siblings or become confidants to an emotionally needy parent or peace-makers in an angry household or super-achievers to distract from addictions in the household. Children who have been family heroes must learn to set limits and allow themselves to be human.

Finally, in some families real abuse takes place. Children are the victims in these families, and as they grow into adulthood they must gain a voice. They must realize they are no longer in the prison of their childhood, recognize that they have choices, and learn to say no to abuse. Then they must gain a voice for themselves, to gain a sense of themselves as worthwhile, respectable, and loved.

Although all three of these movements are about growing up, the work is extremely different for pampered children, heroes, and victims. The central nature of your homework for this stage is what each rewrite must address and what every step forward advances.

Chapter 8

Finding Your Brain: Children Grow Up

*L*earning to think and act for ourselves can be hard when we have competent, caring parents who have helped us every step of the way. Yet sooner or later, like all birds from their nests, children must leave and fly on their own. Those families that provide the most substantial roots for their children often have to work hardest at giving them wings of freedom and responsibility, the subject in fact of a whole book of mine, *Mothers Who Love Too Much.* The spoiled son must learn to do his laundry, the emotionally supported daughter must learn to coach herself, the angry boy must learn civilized conversation about lost luggage, and the shy daughter must learn to walk out on an aggressive date. Although some children never do grow up or are only forced to grow up once their parents die, the goal in parenting is for children to become adults who can stand and talk on their own.

Adult children who are still in many ways pampered and cared for by their parents have the hardest time thinking and acting for themselves on visits home to see family. When parents are so very competent and dominant that their children never quite feel good enough, the children have a hard time realizing they are adults because they are not superstars like their parents. They may, in fact, be quite competent in their jobs and marriages and even as parents, but put them back in the nest and they shrink right down to child-size attitudes and behavior. If being an adult is hard, the place that it is hardest is with the family in which you are forever positioned as the child. Yet this is the place where, if you are able to act like an adult, you will feel finally grown up at last. It is the Olympic race, the stadium where your relational skills are put to their greatest test.

How Children Grow Up

I have watched a fair number of children who are adults grow up in relation to their parents and begin to enjoy family friendships. A number of steps are crucial in that process.

Take Responsibility

When I was at college, I learned to wash my own laundry. I even had to use quarters in machines a long way from my dorm rather than a free machine in the basement of my parents' house. I also had to buy toilet paper for my bathroom, dust and sweep (once a semester at least seemed sufficient), and clean up after myself. Yet when I visited my parents, I reverted back to old ways of expecting them to do things for me. Sure, I might offer to help occasionally, but basically they were responsible and I was the child. Then I would complain that, when I went home, emotionally everything seemed to revert as well.

Eventually I realized that one step of moving past child relationships is to act the adult part with your parents. Practical physical steps are a good beginning place followed by emotional and relational steps.

> **for personal reflection**
>
> *In what ways do you continue to act like a child when you visit your family?*

We all realize at some point that our parents will not be able to carry on their activities or care for us as they have. But why wait until necessity requires it? Why not more gracefully make the transition through a longer period of adult friendship rather than only a shifting of who cares for whom in a crisis.

A first step of adult responsibility that helped in my visits from Houston to my parents in Virginia came when we were able to rent a car rather than having them pick us up at the airport. With two children of our own, we had long since stopped expecting friends whom we visited to pick us up. Why not extend that sense of independence to family? This lessened their burden of providing for our transportation but also gave us new independence in our visits. With my husband's parents, we realized at a certain point that we also needed to stay somewhere other than their home. Their house was too small, and staying there burdened them unnecessarily as they became less physically energetic. Staying elsewhere enabled us to visit in a way that gave us much more equal footing and care for each other.

Other activities for changing relationships have included my moving beyond asking if I can help a little with a meal to taking responsibility for the meal or going to the grocery store and buying food during our visits, doing our family's laundry while visiting (and throwing in some of theirs), and even helping out with their ongoing chores. For children who are used to being well cared-for and parents who enjoy doing things for their children, these changes take conscious effort. But they shift relationships from caregiver adults and pampered children to adults together in a family that allows for a maturing of relationships.

As the three daughters of my parents grew up, got married, and had children, we rarely congregated all together anymore, instead seeing each other in smaller family groups. However, this past summer we were going to be in Virginia all at the same time, and a reunion seemed natural. As we approached it, we remembered earlier visits with everyone: how hectic they were, how anxious mother was, how overwhelming it could be. We realized if we gathered as children and grandchildren expecting my mother to host us all, chaos and anxiety would predominate over fun and relaxation. So we took the bull by the horns and decided to take a responsibility leap forward. My sister and I took on the meals for the weekend, and two of the three families planned to sleep at a nearby cabin rather than my parents' home. My mother enjoyed it so much she wrote a journal of the days, calling it the first annual reunion.

An interesting thing has happened as I have tried to visit as an adult. I had been bothered by how anxious and frenetic my mother often seemed, which made a relaxing vacation hard. As I have begun to take on responsibility and handle more things, my mother has been able to relax and enjoy us more, too. I may have more physical work, but I have received a much more important emotional gift, which is a mother who is more relaxed and able to have fun. That is worth it.

If you come from a family in which your parents

have taken care of you and have taken on lots of the responsibilities in the family, a family that allows you to stay a child into adulthood, at least around them, I encourage you to think of one small responsibility that you can take on in the next visit with your parents. It may simply mean taking out the trash or it could mean tackling all the dinner dishes for a change. You might try something a little bolder like initiating a plan for an activity or taking on the meals for a weekend.

Gain Stature

We physically grow up but don't always take on that full size in our ways of relating to family. Often old patterns that were initiated when we were children remain in our adult visits. Remembering them, we must work to gain emotional height when we visit our family as adults.

One woman who grew up as the younger sister of two brothers was the only one in the family who ever expressed much emotion and so was seen as the crybaby. She sat through family conversations and rarely spoke up but would burst into tears when the tension or hurt became too great for her. As an adult, she had to work to actually speak the words that went with the emotions she had only expressed through tears growing up. She had to recognize that her feelings were not only valid but probably were so intense because they expressed the emotions of the whole family. Gaining stature meant moving away from the crying, sensitive baby sister to a mature adult woman who could put words to her perspective.

As the baby of the family, a man had watched his older sister during adolescence get run over by his domineering mother, leaving him feeling paralyzed, scared, and without a voice. He certainly did not want to jump into the fray and get pounced on himself. Yet he felt intensely the pain of parent-teen fights with his older sister. As an adult businessman, he found himself avoiding conflicts rather than addressing them. In his family, he tended to watch rather than wrestle with difficulties. Gaining stature for him meant learning to tackle the conflicts at work and speaking his feelings and opinions in his family.

For each of us, there are different settings in which we can gain stature. For some it is in carving the Thanksgiving turkey or cooking the pumpkin pies; for others it is directing dinner conversation or deciding when to leave a bad situation. Wherever it is for you that you tend to shrink, think about how you can stand tall and speak up (or hold your tongue if that is what maturity in your family requires) on your next family visit.

Act Mature

A capable director of a not-for-profit center turns suddenly into a young child who goes into temper tantrums at her sister's teasing when she returns home to visit her family. Her blood boils, her nails come out, and she responds with caustic, sarcastic comments when her sister begins the subtle put-downs she has endured all her life. Part of her growing up has been acting her age, acting her status, acting her general level of emotional maturity even in the presence of her sister and mother.

Another woman I know reverts to clothes-tearing, name-calling fights with her sister and mother even though she would never do such a thing at work, with friends, or even with a boyfriend. At a certain point we must look at ourselves as we do children who are not so young but have just regressed into a toddler temper tantrum and say, "Grow up." In fact, it can be helpful to draw upon the voices of our calmest, best teachers and coaches who have encouraged us to "use your words," "ask nicely for what you want," "ignore the person who is acting immature," and "clean up after yourself." We must bring them along as our own inner coach to help us grow up.

Think about the situations that tend to set you off, throw you into childish re-actions, or shrink you emotionally. Now imagine how you would like to act in that situation, with a host of friends cheering you on. What warning lights can be there to keep you from running aground? In what ways can you avoid the old emotional land mines? Plan a

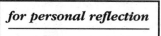

for personal reflection

Think of things you do as an adult in relationships. How might you carry these mature behaviors into your family setting?

growing-up scene in your mind for the next family holiday visit and then see if you can live it out.

When Children Grow Up

My friend Rose has four sons who are a bit older than mine. She worked hard to not be the waitress and maid of the whole family of men, teaching them instead to wash their own clothes and cook some of their own meals. When one of her sons got married, his mother-in-law seemed always rather critical of Winnie as a mother for not catering and caring in her manner of parenting.

Tension continued underneath the surface between these two mothers until one Mother's Day, when Winnie got a call from her son's mother-in-law.

The woman began complimenting Winnie on her wonderful job as a parent. Winnie, a bit amazed, asked further about what was going on. The mother-in-law replied, "Your son just cooked me a wonderful Mother's Day meal." The benefits of having grown-up, competent children had finally struck home.

Chapter 9

Finding Your Heart: Heroes Become Human

Some children, far from being pampered by parents who take special care, are forced to grow up too fast. They fill in for the gaps of their parents, becoming little mothers (or fathers) to younger siblings, trying to keep peace between warring parents, or becoming stars to distract from family distress. Families, like nations, need heroes during times of crisis simply to survive. But humans who try to maintain a permanent hero role pay a price—and so do their families. A hero does more than one normally expects, going beyond typical measures of success and care for others. For an adult who had to play the role of hero in the family as a child, growing up may actually look more like growing down. Growing up means coming to terms with the unrealistic roles and expectations, realizing they cannot and should not do as much as they have been. It means learning to give up heroic goals, never rightly theirs in the first place.

I have never commanded an army in war, rescued

a drowning child, nor pioneered in space, but I have an idea of what being a hero and the humanizing of a hero feels like. Although in many ways I was a pampered child that needed to learn to grow up and take responsibility, in other ways I took on some hero roles. Although mine was always a caring, involved family, my mother's crisis when I was quite small resulted in our learning to be careful about the stress we put on her. Once she came through the crisis, we were eager to put together a happy, normal family again. Unconsciously, I believe, we became fearful of pushing her too far. I picked this up in my father's words to her, "Now don't you be a-worrying" and his careful avoidance of an argument regardless of who might be right or have something to say. For each of the three daughters, the routine question "Did you get 100 in spelling?" perhaps began as a bit of a joke but reflected some truth. And each of us in fact did get 100s in not only spelling but almost everything else.

> *for personal reflection*
>
> **Describe your memories of scenes from childhood where you played the hero.**

This work for excellence and pleasing, while rewarding in many ways, led to a point in my late thirties where I was juggling way too many balls trying to be superwoman. Like the emperor who suddenly realized he had been parading with no clothes, I one day recognized the silliness of juggling so much while enjoying so little. My hero hit the humus of life when my third child was conceived just as we were moving to a new city and renovating an old, historic home. Depressed by the dirt and drudgery, I reached my limits and had to wrestle with them.[4] Out of the darker quiet, I actually learned to wait and be still and surprisingly found new, wonderful life in the listening.

I have helped others who were much more skilled heroes than I to step down from their family pedestals to become their more human, humorous, and life-giving selves over the long term. In doing so, they have discovered parts of themselves and joys in life that they had never had time or freedom to experience before.

John came to see me because of a recent panic attack. He explained that his life was really quite wonderful—fabulous job, lovely wife, two small, happy children—and he just wanted some help with these panic attacks. As we explored his life a bit, it became clear that his great personal success had been fueled by an intense desire to escape the poverty and unpredictability of his childhood. His father had forced his mother into marriage, drank heavily, and often yelled or hit them when he drank. John's mother tried desperately to care for her children but suffered from bouts of depression that left him holding her up emotionally. His light came from great performance at school and attention of teachers who praised him. So he did well, really really well, went to a top college and graduate school and got into a good investment firm, settled far from home, married, and had two children. All seemed well except that his feelings were so locked up in the chest of his past that he was not able to feel much—pain or joy. And the bottling up was coming out in frightening panic attacks. John was paying a high price for being the hero, not only in the panic attacks but in a life that had become focused on avoiding difficulty and keeping things neat.

He would have liked a quick fix, a quick word, or pills, but as he did the harder work of opening the

Pandora's box of his past, which was now at a relatively safe distance, he found an unexpected benefit. In the process of sorting through old feelings, he was able to unload the heavy emotional pack he'd been carrying and was able to lower some of his tight defenses against his feelings. He related at one meeting some unexpected benefits from his emotional work. He had begun to talk to an elderly neighbor, listen to his woes, and share his own daily discouragements in a way that actually brought them both rays of hope. He noted how he was playing and laughing with his children more freely and wasn't so impatient with them when they fell apart in tears. He talked of concern for abused children and identified a desire to become involved in a charity organization. His internal wall against allowing himself to feel began to slowly melt, and like the Tin Woodsman he found himself gaining a heart.

Characteristics of Heroes

Heroes usually begin with natural talents—intelligence, determination, athletic prowess, musical gifts, patience. But in a family with difficulties, they become highlighted and called upon in unnatural ways.

for personal reflection

In what ways do you continue to act as a hero with your family?

This may happen because a father is so harsh and driven that a son forces all his effort into athletic success. Or a mother may be depressed or absent so an intelligent or emotionally sensitive daughter takes over the mothering of siblings. Or a parent may be alcoholic but a child's great performance can keep the family from focusing on the drinking problem. Or a capable young boy is told he must be the man of the house when his father leaves. As they realize their family's need for these talents, the heroes work even harder to avoid the disaster that failure would bring and to keep gaining the praise. Their success and the family's response to them becomes self-reinforcing.

Tasks for the Humanizing of Heroes

Several transformations can be undergone to turn heroes into humans. Let's examine them.

Recognize Costs
Heroes rarely give up their heroics until they realize how much they cost. These costs come out in different ways and at different times in peoples' lives.

- John was paying the price not only of panic attacks but the dulling of all of his emotions in the need to keep from feeling pain.

- Arthur escaped life with a mother who was totally unpredictable and a father who beat him unmercifully by becoming a top salesman with his company, a leading Sunday school teacher, and an involved dad. His cost came out in periodic crippling depressions that needed more than passing attention.

- Sally had played the hero daughter for years for her parents, who never seemed quite satisfied with her appearance or performance. She had given up boyfriends whom they did not like (all of them), she had not gone to graduate school, and she had not bought her own house, all in hopes of pleasing them one day. In effect, she had given up the life she wanted to lead and still never gained their acceptance.

- Barbara played the hero by catering to whatever her mother needed when Barbara visited her and by doing the things she felt her mother should do—making meals, washing the dog, even cleaning toilets. However, she and her mother paid a high price in an ever simmering anger and constant sense of judgment that Barbara carried with her toward her mother. This anger spilled over to other relationships and to boyfriends as she developed friendships in which she also felt not understood and taken advantage of.

- Bill paid the price of never having time to enjoy his life. He worked so hard at building his own company and being a responsible father that he never sat down to relax, went out to play golf, or just took a down day. With no "white space" in his active life, he wasn't enjoying the many things he was doing and operated more out of guilt and pride than real passion and joy.

Often heroes don't stop until they develop an overwhelming symptom, such as panic attacks, depression, pending divorce, or anger that drives away relationships. But if you recognize your own tendency to be the family hero, you can listen and look for the price you may be paying before it mounts up into such a catastrophic payment. Listen to your body, listen to your feelings, don't put them aside and order yourself around anymore. Instead, pay attention. Be careful to observe warning signals, including headaches, feeling overwhelmed, self-doubts, and simmering anger. When the needle on the dash of my car begins to move toward *H* from *C*, I often don't notice it. If I do, I hope it will just go back down soon. But invariably the red light comes on and if I ignore that, one day I will have smoke rising from the hood in the middle of the freeway. So, too, with the emotional build-up that comes from being the hero. I suggest you check the engine, slow down, and add water when you notice the needle rising.

Set Limits

Heroes do not have accurate personal gauges as to what they can and cannot do. They have learned to push themselves to, often beyond, their limits. They don't know what normal human expectations are. Instead of listening to their bodies and emotions, they command them. Once heroes begin to realize the price they are paying and the pains they are feeling, the next step is to set limits to lessen that pain and give up the heroic acts.

One family hero, after a tough divorce while just getting back on her feet in terms of a job and relationships, got a call from her mother who announced she was coming to visit to get away from her own hassles at home. The hero accepted her mother's coming but let her know that she could not give up her whole schedule on a moment's notice. So her mother came, but the hero went about her business and did not respond to the pattern of guilt that would have in earlier days led her to cancel dates and run herself ragged to take her mother around the town.

The hero who took over housecleaning and cooking for her parents on visits home has begun to go for a more relaxed visit and sit on her hands to keep from doing all the dirty work that leaves the house clean but the relationships filled with anger.

Setting limits can be guided by physical symptoms, such as a need for rest or food or quiet. Emotional levels of anger or depression can be the guide for saying no to heroic chores and yes to more life-giving activities. If you are a hero, remember that your family may enjoy what you do for them but neither you nor they enjoy it enough to endure your resentment or scorn. So give up the heroics, become more human, and you may enjoy yourself more. And your family may feel more capable by comparison.

Ask for Help

A step beyond setting limits is asking for help. Getting a hero to ask for help is much like expecting a tadpole to walk. Fortunately, tadpoles can turn into frogs and heroes can learn to be human. When someone comes to my house for dinner and asks to help, I have always typically responded, "Oh no, I'm fine." Of course, I am running ragged inside but somehow feel the perfect hostess does it all herself and graciously. I gained a lot from watching a friend of mine, a priest who makes Jesus much more human for me. Whenever I visit and ask to help, she takes me up on it, handing me potatoes to peel or a stack of plates to put out. Sometimes she even asks for help without my offering. And she does not apologize for not being able to do it all herself. This ability of hers makes me feel relaxed in her presence because pretense is gone and our roles are level. As a result, sharing is more natural.

Heroes are often the hosts or hostesses at family gatherings, or they take the major responsibility for everything happening. Asking others to help may be humbling if you are used to playing a role that depends on your gaining praise for

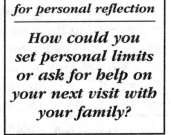

for personal reflection

How could you set personal limits or ask for help on your next visit with your family?

heroics, but it will usually mean much more pleasant relationships for all. If you are the one who comes away from family gatherings exhausted from buying and wrapping all the presents or cooking all the meals or making peace between all the warring parties, take a careful look before the next holiday. Decide what you will not do and then what you will ask others to do. Even small requests can make a big difference in your own attitude and that of family members. At your next family gathering, consider eating humble pie by asking someone else to make the pumpkin pie. You may enjoy the vacation while they feel great that they can contribute.

Accept Parents' Limits

Just because you are giving up some of the practices of the hero does not mean that suddenly your parents, or other family members, will become more capable. They probably have their own real limits or illnesses that may have been what got the whole hero role started. Occasionally others step up to the plate when you back down, grateful that they finally have a chance to make a hit. But often they continue—limited, bumbling, constrained as always.

Your choice is to continue being angry, trying to change them (usually to no avail), or to come to terms with their limits. All parents fall short of our hopes for them to be all-loving and all-knowing. Like the Wizard of Oz, they cannot fulfill our grand hopes. Seeing them as human, with their set of difficulties and challenges, can help us to move on in our own responsibilities and relationships.

Beyond the realization of their limits, the inner spiritual work of forgiveness is needed to free you from ongoing resentment. You may need to identify the specific instances in which you felt let down or hurt as well as the larger ways they have not been all you wanted and needed. The heart work of forgiveness is hardest but most profound when we wrestle with our feelings toward those we know the best, who possibly love us most but have also most deeply hurt us or let us down.

> *for personal reflection*
>
> **What are your parents' limitations? What do you miss getting from them?**

Broaden Your Support Base

Even the best of parents cannot be all things to each child. This is why many faiths give a prominent role to godparents, why families need involved grandparents, and why Hillary Clinton wrote about the village it takes to raise a child. Rather than forever focusing on what a certain person or family member is not, we must as adults seek out mentors, coaches, and friends who can fill in the broad base of support we need to move forward. When parents are particularly limited or even harmful in their behaviors, we have a bigger gap to fill. So we must seek even harder for people whom we admire, who have qualities our parents lack, and who can be adopted as emotional parents for us.

My good friend Heidi had a challenging family situation growing up. Her mother was limited in the emotional security she could provide, with my friend becoming more of the mother in the family. She knew early on that she was lacking in mothering herself. So she sought, found, latched onto, and kept a variety of older women and peers who have provided the extra mothering she needed. Heidi always wears a set of bangle bracelets. Once I asked her curiously about these, for they are a trademark on her wrist. She explained that they are her "mother bracelets." Each was given by or represents one of these women in her life: her own mother, an adopted mother from college years, and a friend who was always there for her. I, too, added to the collection as we now jointly mother one another. I have adopted her way of accumulating significant relationships that support and encourage me. My mother is one, but to that foundation I have added many friends who have helped correct and carry me these many years.

Recently I was about to make a trip to Cochabamba, Bolivia, to visit the orphans and staff that are part of a mission I love and support.[5] I had a particular connection and sense of gratitude to the mamas, each of whom cares day in and day out for ten children. I wondered how in

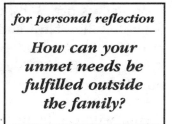

for personal reflection

How can your unmet needs be fulfilled outside the family?

the world I could express my appreciation to them. Suddenly I realized what I would bring them: a mother bracelet. I had just purchased for my own birthday a beautiful silver bracelet encircled with various faith symbols to finally have my own mother bracelet. I knew I must also get one for each of these Bolivian adoptive mothers to our mission children. Shortly thereafter, I was sitting around the table of La Morada, the mission retreat house in Bolivia, sharing my special idea, only to find out there was one new mama for whom I did not have a bracelet. I was discouraged, but then realized I had an extra, the one on my arm. So the next day, sitting around the laundry room/gathering room with all the staff, I shared Heidi's story and then gave a mother bracelet to each mama: Francisca, Jesusa, Maria, Marina, and Lucy.

Several days after I returned, I got a package in the mail. I opened it to discover a gift for myself: a silver bracelet with symbols and a note, "From a mother who loves you." I did not know at that moment whom it was from, imagining it representing love from my mother, my friends who have mothered me, and God who has filled all the gaps and made firm the gracious comforting arms of love. It confirmed the full circle of our always receiving back when we give away. Heroes have a hard time receiving but when they allow it to happen, the joy and relief is deep. I discovered later that Heidi had sent it after hearing my story. But she—like our parents who give whatever they have and like those who must add more to fill our emotional cups—only manifests through her love the larger gift of God who must fill our deepest wells.

Chapter 10

Finding Your Courage: Victims Gain Voices

*I*magine a four-year-old whose father comes home in a drunken rage, an eight-year-old whose mother beats her for not having dinner ready when she gets home from work, or a heartbroken ten-year-old whose father commands her to stop crying over friends left behind in a move. As children, they cannot leave home, for their parents are their only source of survival, even if they are their emotional torment as well.

But when the four- or eight- or ten-year-old grows up, he or she becomes physically free and often looks for any chance to leave home just to escape the pain. As an adult, the daughter or son from such a tormented home is no longer unable to leave. Their size and voice have grown to match their parents'. Yet the pattern of being a victim often remains with them and at no time more than when they visit their parents and revert back to childlike helplessness. This is not the helplessness of pampered children who sink back into having mom serve them cookies and milk and do their laundry. This is the helplessness of fear and pain and emotional prison. The challenge for those coming from such families is to gain strength and freedom, both physical and emotional, so that as adult children they go home prepared with feet to walk out of abusive scenes, a voice to speak against injustice, and compassion for the many wounds, both of themselves and their parents.

Emotional abuse and neglect can be wrapped in beautiful paper and bows. Families in which the underlying feeling is of great pain can live in lovely homes, go to church, act nicely to neighbors and friends, and seem to be upstanding community citizens. Sometimes, like alcoholics, they deteriorate enough that they become a bum living under the freeway, but more often families with these great pains still look good to those outside. So victims suffer not only the actual hurts but also the confusion that comes from a sense of others not knowing their pain. They alone know what core feelings they have about their families and what the real scenes are in their memories from holidays in the past.

If your gut feelings are about these painful experiences as a childhood victim, acknowledge and wrestle with them honestly, for only in so doing can you experience new patterns for family visits.

Those who have been deeply wounded through neglect or abuse by their parents feel the greatest sense of dread, guilt, and sadness around visits to family. Usually they hate returning to the scene of the crime. Often the patterns continue—of not listening, of drinking getting worse, of anger raging on. Even if parents have mellowed, simply being with them or in places of old hurts brings back painful memories. Yet children continue pilgrimages home, out of guilt for not tending to aging parents, hope that maybe they will one day get the love that has never come, or simply out of habit. Going home for the holidays is especially hard because of the awful memories of those same holidays from the past compounded by the societal expectations for happy family holidays.

Though the pain is greatest and the work most difficult, adult children from these families have the most to gain from changing family patterns. Hope comes not from changing your parents but from the possibility of gaining the courage to no longer tolerate abuse, to stand up for what you need, and to create new patterns within the new family you are building for yourself.

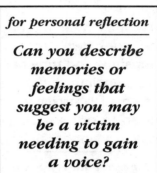

for personal reflection

Can you describe memories or feelings that suggest you may be a victim needing to gain a voice?

Learn to Listen to Your Soul

When you grow up in an unsafe, unpredictable environment, you become like a scared rabbit or a tyrant's soldier, attuned to every noise and movement outside yourself that might represent danger. Danger may come in the form of a father who has had a bad day and is ready to lash out or a mother who is depressed and cannot handle one more need or a parent whose expectations are coupled with harsh consequences for failure. So your ears are well trained to the outer world. But your internal hearing is often not developed or is severely impaired. Victims often do not know exactly what they are feeling, presenting instead just a mass of depression or anxiety or self-doubt. A first step forward is learning to listen to your inner feelings to unravel the strings one by one so that they can be useful guides for growing.

If you have grown up more attuned to the needs of others or the threats you needed to avoid, then your adult growth will include the development of the inner ear to your soul. You must learn to listen to yourself, not discount your feelings or hopes, and use your own discernment as a guide to your relationships and direction in life.

An ancient but simple spiritual discipline, the examen of conscience, can be helpful in learning to listen to one's soul. This is presented in a modern way in a wonderful little book, *Sleeping with Bread*.[6]

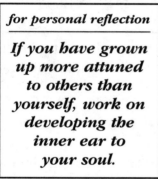

for personal reflection

If you have grown up more attuned to others than yourself, work on developing the inner ear to your soul.

The authors suggest at the end of the day you ask yourself two questions: For what was I most grateful? and For what am I least grateful? Considered on a regular basis, these questions can help you identify the movements of hope and discouragement. They can help you find the destructive sources to say no to and the sources of life to say yes to.

As you learn to listen to your soul, several steps must be taken in relationships and visits with your family. First, you must say no to abuse. Second, you must plan your visits with family carefully.

Say No to Abuse

As you begin to listen to your soul, a first voice to hear is the one that calls abuse by its real name.

Lobsters are often put in a pot of cold water that is then gradually heated up, to boiling and death. They don't realize the change in temperature because it is so gradual. So, too, children who have grown up with abuse do not recognize what is going on, especially when parents also are loving, caring, and good intentioned in other ways. When you are yelled at regularly, you become numb to yelling. When you have had to take care of yourself from an early age, you don't expect people to care for you.

We all tend to think that what goes on in our families is what happens in all families. However, on a gut level we all recognize certain things as painful and wrong. So the first step is to listen to that inner voice, to acknowledge our pain, to be clear about what we don't like and what we do not want to continue into adulthood and especially not into our ongoing family visits.

Even if you feel the abuser did not intentionally hurt you (most parents do not set out to hurt their children; they think they are doing the best thing for their children even when they cause great hurt) or had problems that caused the situation, you must begin by acknowledging clearly your experience. Once you recognize what is abusive at worst or what you personally dislike at best, you as an adult can say no to it in a variety of ways.

One friend's mother always points out her weight to her in a way that demeans and belittles her. Occasionally, she gives a direct insult like "You look like a slob" or "No wonder you aren't married, with all that weight," but more often she demeans in subtle ways, such as giving her daughter clothes a size too small. Saying no for this daughter meant, after thirty-five years of saying nothing, finally speaking directly to her mother about the pain of these criticisms and asking her to stop such put-downs. The follow-through meant sometimes saying, "Mother, if you bring up my weight, I will not want to talk with you and won't be calling you until I'm feeling a lot stronger."

Another friend grew up with a father who was a successful, esteemed doctor but at home was a progressive alcoholic. Standard fare around the dinner table included his ignoring the women, talking with the men, and making snide remarks to his wife and daughter. When this daughter returned home to visit her father with her own daughters, the same patterns persisted. However, now as an adult she gained the courage to speak up and say, "Dad, that's really not an appropriate comment" or "That's a rather rude comment for the dinner table, don't you think?" or "I don't see it that way at all." Although her inner fears were similar to those she had as a child, she learned to speak up as an adult, leave the table (or house) if necessary, avoid private places that risked greater abuse, and do whatever else was needed to ensure that visits did not include abusive actions or language.

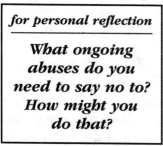

for personal reflection

What ongoing abuses do you need to say no to? How might you do that?

Learning to say no to abuse can be extremely scary and difficult, given the emotional and sometimes real power of the abuser. However, once done, it is incredibly empowering for an adult who as a child felt so helpless. Every step toward speaking up and standing up adds height, security, and confidence to a previously frightened inner child. And it gives that adult huge amounts of confidence and power for speaking up in other life situations.

Plan Limited Visits Carefully

When you know that your parent has certain behaviors that can go out of control or become intolerable to you, it's important to plan visits in a way that gives you room to stop the behavior toward you or leave the scene should they occur. This is true with a parent whose drinking is out of control, who rages unpredictably, or who belittles you unmercifully. But it is also true any time you know there is an interaction or set of behaviors that are going to affect you so much that you lose your own sense of self and personal control.

Once we go over the edge with our own anger, depression, or anxiety, constructive relating is almost impossible. Your parent may be acting in a way that friends or casual acquaintances find perfectly acceptable but that triggers for you terribly strong emotions (perhaps because of the earlier scenes that they recall or because of the intensity of your relationship with your parent). What should guide you is not simply external standards of appropriate behavior but your own internal reactions.

When you are visiting family, be sure to take along not just your toothbrush and shoes but your personal thermostat of your inner anger, depression, or anxiety. Be alert to what is happening within you before it goes out of control. I often ask clients to imagine a scale from one to ten for their level of feeling. This may be experienced primarily as anger, depression, or anxiety. Then I ask them to become aware of where they are throughout the day. Many people only notice what is happening when they reach the nine or ten level, which means they are about to blow up, have sunk terribly low, or are about to have an anxiety attack. The key is to pay attention much earlier to what is happening to your emotions so that as you move from six to seven or eight you can begin to address your needs. Regardless of how great or how minor the difficult behavior of another person, you alone are responsible for being aware of how you are feeling and taking steps to change or control yourself when you feel yourself moving beyond control.

In planning your visits home, be realistic about how long you can be with family and remain a pleasant and capable adult. You may be able to stay under the same roof for a month at a time or you may only be able to handle a one-hour meal in a restaurant. This may be the most crucial step in planning—realistic assessment of how long and where the family can visit in a constructive way so as to not set up yourself or your own family. It doesn't matter what you or others think you or they should be able to handle. What matters is what is actually possible. Then plan around that reality. Better a short visit that is enjoyable or at least tolerable than a longer visit that produces more hurt and resentment.

> *for personal reflection*
>
> **What are concrete ways that you can avoid reaching the top ten on the stress scale during a visit?**

Say Yes to Life

In your life as a whole, the ear of your soul needs to be listening for the signs of life. What has kept you going, what nourishes your soul, what makes you laugh, what gives you energy? Look for the life-giving events and relationships in your life. Learn to pay attention to these in everyday life and you will be able to create them in your visits home as well.

For me, the sky offers soul nurture—not only spectacular sunsets or quiet sunrises but light peeking through dark clouds, animal pictures in the clouds, and the azure blue of the turning from night to day. The sounds of the frog fountain in my garden, the feel of warm and alive skin in a hug from my seven-year-old, a cup of Starbucks café mocha are also little signs of life to me. When I return home to Virginia, I realize I need to sneak out in the morning for quiet and nature's nurturing, whether on the spectacular hilltop at the farm, a walk around the city park near my parents' house, or just a quiet time in the hammock in the backyard. I also need quality one-on-one time to talk, not just interrupted chaotic mingling. What gives you life, in the everyday? in your visits home? Listen for them, seek them out, carve them out in your visits home so you are a more alive, positive person within the family.

Fishing in a beautiful spot, reading a funny children's book, dancing wildly, going to the farmer's market, and sipping a cup of tea are some of the nurturing sources of life to victims I have counseled. They have learned to give these treats to themselves and seek them out as regular routines in their lives. When they visit family, they take these routines with them or find substitute activities to alleviate the stress of these visits. When they manage to do so, they change slowly from de-

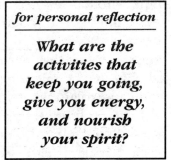

for personal reflection

What are the activities that keep you going, give you energy, and nourish your spirit?

defended, angry, or proud family members into more relaxed, honest, caring members of the family.

Build New Family

Our parents, unfortunately, are humans . . . and limited even at that. They bear their own wounds that keep them from giving more or being more. Children who unveil the wizard must find ways to journey toward wholeness and home without relying on the wizard who is no wizard at all. When you feel more like a victim than a spoiled child, you must seek out others to fill in the circle of parenting for you. Like the heroes who must broaden their own support base, victims must use their voices to find and ask others to pick up for them where their parents have left off. They must add the bangle bracelets of other mothers and fathers to provide the love and support and free space that their own parents could not give.

No one can choose their natural parents. But as adults we can choose our mentors and friends, and we are responsible for how we do that. In my front garden hangs a plaque from one of those friends of mine who has learned this lesson: "Friends are chosen family." You might have sometimes secretly thought, "I wish _____ was my parent." If so, you can go to that person or someone similar and ask if he or she might be a friend or support to you. You can explain what you admire about him or her and how you are trying to grow. You can assemble around yourself those people whom you would like to be like and learn from. Rather than remaining resentful, angry, or guarded all your life, you can as an adult create your own family by asking for and investing in the sorts of relationships you have always wanted. The process is slow, but—over time—transformation and new life will blossom.

Come to Life

Jill once described to me in some detail incidents from a book she had just read of the horrid, tortured life of a child. Then she turned to me with her face tensed and explained that her own growing up felt like such torment. Her work to say no to abuse and yes to life has been long and laborious.

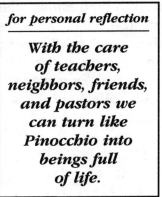

for personal reflection

With the care of teachers, neighbors, friends, and pastors we can turn like Pinocchio into beings full of life.

One day, as she was reflecting on her memories from the past, her eyes glazed a bit and then lit up as she recalled one wonderful experience of hope in the midst of a rather frightening childhood. She described how she loved reading, over and over, the story of *Pinocchio.* She described the smell of the breeze from the window and the feel of the cushioned chair she would sit in to read. Then she told me of the almost mystical feeling she would experience as she read about the magical moment when the carved wooden puppet suddenly turned into a live boy. Listening to her, I felt as if I was experiencing a bit of that very transformation happening in my office. Here was a girl whose parents gave her only the rough wooden form of human life, who by her own heart efforts to listen for life and say no to past wrongs was before my eyes turning into a living, feeling, dancing woman.

Sometimes the only thing our parents can give us is a rough wooden carving. Beyond that, their physical or financial or emotional reserves are so depleted that they offer us no breath of real life. Yet, with the care and love of teachers, neighbors, friends, counselors, pastors, and with a seeking heart, we can turn like Pinocchio into living beings full of spirit, capable of great adventures far beyond any wild dreams of our parents. Those whom I see who are most victimized in their family lives have the deepest pain and greatest ongoing challenge in their visits home. But they also have the greatest potential for movement and coming to life. When they gain their voice to sing, the song comes from a passion and joy at finding life, and the sound is often richer than any other.

Creating Your Own Home

Once we are old enough to go home as adults, we are old enough to be building our own homes. We move beyond adolescent critique to the opportunity and responsibility we share as adults in society. We have, it is hoped, learned from watching our parents, their strengths and failings. Now it is our turn to try our hand at home making. In doing so, we must face the emotional and relational tasks left to our generation and explore the process of our own home building, establishing rituals that will keep us alive and growing.

Chapter 11

This Generation's Work

*E*very Sunday afternoon I make my way with my guitar to St. James's Church. There an assorted gathering of transients from the streets of Houston are treated to an afternoon meal and the preaching of Tony Campbell. Tony once described a crucial day in his track career during college. He was on the relay team, running for Navy against West Point. The teams were within a few points in the track meet totals at the start of the relay, so the winner of this race would win the meet. Tony was third in the four-man relay, and he watched anxiously as the first two runners raced around the course, each losing more ground. By the time the baton was passed to Tony, his team was twenty-four meters behind and seemed destined to lose. Nevertheless, he put all his strength and will into his lap, gaining eight meters of lost ground but still too far behind for a winning race. He passed the baton to his anchor man, Daryl Anderson, went out in the middle of the field, and pulled his sweat clothes over his head in despair. A few minutes later he began to hear the crowd cheer. He looked up to see Daryl, who had run what seemed beyond human ability, pulling ahead of West Point. He crossed the finish line just ahead of West Point, and the crowd went wild. Tony jumped from his slouched grief to unbelieving joy.

A relay race, with many legs run by different members' handing off a common baton until they reach the end, is the story of our family lives. As we move from generation to generation, we are in a grand relay. Sometimes the people in the legs ahead of us have run so beautifully and so hard that they allow us to start with a giant lead, handing us the baton from a family that has given us a great foundation. This may give us great confidence but it may also make us wonder if we can keep such an outstanding lead. Sometimes the runners have just run their steady best and want us to keep that up. Sometimes the people in the legs ahead of us fall way behind. They may veer off course, be sick and run poorly, or develop a cramp in their leg and collapse. We don't have a lot of say about how the people ahead of us have run. In a relay race we simply must take the baton where we receive it, run our lap the best we can, and hand it off to the next person, who must take it across the finish line.

We are born with different parents: some are emotional track stars, others are average parenting runners, and still others collapse in the middle of the race. By virtue of our birth, we are in this generational family race and by virtue of our death will be handing the baton on to others, whether they are our children or those we nurture in other ways.

The Lap before Us

I sometimes have been critical of my mother's giving

all her energy to raise her children and not having many friends, interests, or career of her own. I have been stopped in my critical tracks when I have realized the great job my mother did to correct the failings of her parents. She was raised with two parents who were so involved with friends and community that they had little time for their children, which left her without a great deal of security and self-confidence. Because of this, she and my father dedicated their time and energy to their children and purposely set aside many of their own interests (which they have now taken up with vigor). They provided us with a home in which we were central, our routines were set, and we knew how special we were. These secure roots have in fact enabled all of us to stretch our wings broadly and confidently. My mother could not do for her children what she wanted to do as well as take on a career of her own. My mother did her work the way she could. Now I must do my generation's work.

Once I suggested a fairly standard beginning remedy to a woman who came to me because her marriage was in trouble. I asked that she and her husband go out on a date once a week to renew the relationship in some positive ways. She looked hesitant and explained that she would not be able to do that because her nine-year-old son could not go to sleep without her there to tuck him in. I began to inquire further and, as I often do when I don't understand a family situation, I went one generation back and asked, "Tell me about your parents." Her face tensed and she shook her head, "My father left when I was small and my mother was out with one man after another, sometimes late into the night. She was never there for us. We raised ourselves . . . and I swore I would be there for my children." Sud-

157

denly I saw her in a different light, no longer the overprotective mother but the faithful, ever-present, loving mother to her son. Her son may have to do some work on developing wings to fly, but this mother had already made a huge gain in family health in her lap thus far.

> **for personal reflection**
>
> *At some point beyond assessing or blaming or thanking those before us, we must realize the baton is in our hands.*

The son I have discussed earlier, whose mother was competent and stable but unaffectionate due to her own traumatic growing up, needed to realize that his mother had done the heroic work of her generation, moving her family from chaos to stability. It was left to him and his sisters to do the work of adding affection and open communication to their relationships in their generation.

Most parents run the best parenting race they can, given their age and maturity, talents and traumas. In fact, if you go back and ask about your parents' own beginnings in the parenting business, they will usually talk about their determination to do things right, and often differently, from their parents. Listening to parents' and grandparents' stories from the previous generations can help children understand the hard work their parents have done, how far they have come, or the tough situations that hindered them.

Recently I was attending my twentieth college reunion in Cambridge with my fifteen-year-old son. He'd gone with me to a Radcliffe forum in which lots of gender issues were discussed. We were talking about how women still end up with the majority of home and child work even if they have a career. I offhandedly said, "Maybe you can improve over your father on that."

He quickly commented, "Yes, but look what an improvement Dad made over his father." He realized this generational work issue better than I did, for he recognized that his father had given so much more in the way of fathering than his grandfather. And we both then commented that probably Grandpa had made a jump from his father.

The Baton Is in Our Hands

The book thus far has dealt with the leg in the family relay race before ours and our hand-off techniques and patterns. We can keep standing on the lead we've been given or complaining about the loss we began with. But at a certain point beyond assessing and blaming or thanking those who have run before us, we must realize that the baton is now in our hands. Our parents have done what they can. Children can always spot where their parents fall short. But the greatest value in such appraisals is not to change one's parents but to determine one's own lap of the race. As we reach adulthood, gain keys to a car and a voter registration card, we also gain a baton for the living of our lives and for the running of our relational lap. When the baton is passed in the emotional relay race, we must carry on.

We Are the World
A frightening thought has come to me as I have grown older and, I hope, wiser. I now look on those who are just out of college or in their twenties and thirties as really young, yet they are the new parents of the world. I often think I am still a kid trying to

figure out what to do with my life and how to handle myself. Yet as my oldest son leaves for college, I realize that all this time I've been trying to figure out how to parent, whatever I've been doing in the meantime is the parenting he actually received. I have been the human, often bumbling, and now aging mother whom he had hoped would be a superhuman.

As adults we are entrusted with momentous tasks: parenting, working, running families and companies and countries. Once a year, my family and I attend a gathering of many leaders from a variety of fields—political, academic, and social—who meet as friends primarily to reflect and share together. I often feel as if I have been invited by accident. Yet I find that most of the people there feel the same way, for most of us are aware of the gap between our real abilities and the impressions others have of our jobs or titles.

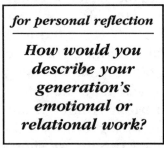

for personal reflection

How would you describe your generation's emotional or relational work?

We gather for some honest conversation and support as humans aware of our limitations while being leaders of our respective fields. It is a frightening yet humbling awareness.

This leadership gathering is for the whole family, and the children who attend with us are greatly valued. They are put on panels with well-known leaders and are given as much esteem (or more) than any of the adults. My son had a realization last year after one of his panels and moaned, "Not many more years can I be on a panel just because of my age. Before long, I'll have to do something notable." Now he knows how we all feel as adults—not quite up to the task and age we have reached. When the baton is handed to us, we are not usually as well trained as we might wish. When the baton of parenting is handed to us by virtue of our having a child (or taking on a parenting role for other's children), whether planned for years at forty or coming as a surprise much earlier, we are in the race and must run however well we can. When the baton is handed to us, we must cheer ourselves on and listen to the voices of those surrounding us: "Run, run your hardest and best, and do it now."

Our Generation's Work

Remembering that our parents have done the best they can and remembering that we are humans and not wizards, we must consider carefully and realistically what is our generation's work. We must choose a relational goal and work to meet it. For me, one goal has been to push past the tendency to seek peace at any price in order to speak up for myself more freely and to address conflicts openly. Also, my work involves finding a personal balance between an enthusiastic "I can do it" and a humble acceptance of my limitations.

One man, whose father was harsh and whose family was chaotic, has a goal to have a stable and loving marriage and family. Simple pleasures of playing ball with his sons, eating family dinners with reasonable discussions, and teaching Sunday school are major accomplishments for him and his children.

The son of the successful, hard-driving father and competent but unaffectionate mother has the goal of learning to take time to smell the roses and relax enough to express affection. The woman whose mother is afraid to do much on her own has a goal of learning to take risks and try new adventures. All goals for our own relational laps depend on the laps of our parents ahead of us, our personal passions and talents, and our goals for our children yet ahead. Our children include not only the children we bear but anyone we care for as teachers, coaches, godparents, mentors, aunts, or uncles. As adults, whether married or single, with no children of our own or ten, we contribute to the next generation. And the work we do is a gain not only for us but for them.

Not Repeating or Reacting

One caution must be observed in running our relational lap. If we do not carefully and thoughtfully do our homework, we may end up repeating our parents' mistakes. Even when we think we are not, our voices will sound the same harsh tones, our patterns in relationships will look all too familiar, and we will find ourselves becoming our parents. We can also end up repeating our parents' mistakes by reacting against our parents in such a way that we go to the opposite extreme. In my case, I tended to react against what I experienced as my mother's reluctance to handle new challenges or take on social activities by cheerfully taking on heroic numbers of tasks with a superwoman approach. Only as I reached age forty did I realize that the danger in my taking on so much was that it produced some of the anxiety and lack of enjoyment of life that I was trying to escape. My real work was not to automatically say, "Sure, I can do that." Rather it was to learn to take things on positively but with some discretion so that I could enjoy them along the way.

Generational Catch-Up Work

In a relay race, the extent of our challenge depends a great deal on how well the team members ahead of us ran. And how well we run will make a difference not just for ourselves but for those who run after us. I work with many people whose family history is filled with trauma. Often a person may be the only one in the family doing the emotional and spiritual work. I am careful to let them know that the work is more difficult because it is done perhaps for a whole generation or several generations. He or she is catching up by addressing issues that were neglected by many people for many years. Yet by doing it, the person keeps it from being passed down to the next generation. The person is unloading the emotional backpack that has been filled with anger and hurt and sadness and dead things for a long time so that the children will not have to carry it as well. Unpacking this emotional baggage is one of the greatest gifts to your children, even though they may never know what you have done or be able to thank you for it. I sometimes give people a choice as they face some hard emotional work. I tell them they can do it themselves or leave it for their children. With that choice, most people opt to do the work themselves so as to leave their children less emotional catch-up work.

Timing the Hand-off

A hand-off occurs when parents die and children become the oldest living generation. Many people wait for this life and death transition before they do their family work or take hold of the baton. I have known several people whose family work never came to a head until a crucial member died. Sometimes it takes the death of a key member for the next generation to wrestle with their roles or be freed to move forward themselves. Others simply hold onto old ways of relating because they are familiar, and they don't think about what comes next until a parent dies. But when a parent dies without having helped the younger members take on adult roles, the shock can be overwhelming.

One woman I know experienced such grief when her father died that her husband said she never recovered her joy in life. Another woman has had a tough time becoming her own coach since she relied so thoroughly on her always present, wise, and supporting mother. When the unresolved emotions are negative, they become more tangled, angry, and guilt-ridden after a death.

Grown-Ups together for a Lap

By going home grown up, you give yourself some years with both parents and children working together as adults, running some of the hand-off lap together. Children learn to run more surely, the hand-off is smoother, the final toss less traumatic when children and parents can be grown-ups together in a family.

My friend Rose, who is a stage ahead of me in family life, has a goal that I would like to aim for. Her sons are grown but she has a target beyond getting them successfully raised or holding onto them after they have become adults. She describes her wish to develop "a family of friends." Indeed, perhaps the greatest tribute to any family member, be it mother or father, sister or brother, is when they can say of one another, "Here is my best friend." Best or not, I will be happy to simply be friends, adult to adult, with as many of my family as possible—my elders, my sisters, and my youngers. For a parent and a child to be friends, the child must take on the responsi-

> **for personal reflection**
>
> **What are your goals for the next generation?**

bility and attitudes of an adult, and the parent must accept the child as a grown member of the community. When this happens, we have the pleasure of running together for a lap.

The Final Lap

Tony Campbell collapsed with a towel over his head after running his lap, sure that despite his best efforts his team would lose the race and the meet. Often, even when we run our best in relationships, we are aware that others are far ahead of us. Sitting despondent in the middle of the field, Tony heard the roar of the crowd as his anchor man came home. He also tells of his relational anchor man that he now trusts in the larger game of life, the God of mercy and grace who alone will eventually bring us home.

We are not God but human, all too young and foolish when we become parents, all too quickly becoming old and gray. We can only run the lap we are given, with whatever energy and creativity and love we can muster. But if we do our generation's work, we will hand off to our children, having caught up a bit emotionally in our lap. Then we must pass the baton on to others who will run after us. The final outcome, however, we must leave in other hands. And I for one believe that the final anchor is not a frail human at all but a God of grace who knows only too well our human limits. Our lap is but one part of a much, much grander game of life that I believe the Creator holds within his love. Tony, telling the story of his relay race, reminds us with his confident voice, "And God alone is our anchor man. He will do what no one else can do, even on the day of our death—he will bring us home."

Chapter 12

Home Making

When as newlyweds we moved into our first apartment on 109th Street in Manhattan's Upper West Side, I had my first home of my own. We brought my husband's oak bed from his family home, picked out a blue-and-brown plaid sofa from Macy's basement, and bought a dining room set secondhand from a man in Brooklyn. I tried out my mother's recipes and pulled out a few new cookbooks as well to prepare our meals. I was decorating, cleaning, cooking like an adult. But I felt in many ways as if I was only playing house. I felt the way I had as a little girl with the plastic stove and ironing board. Yet I was actually married, and no one was offering dinner when the game got tiring or messed up. This was my house, and I was the real adult in it. Even twenty years later, I sometimes feel more as though I am playing house than being a real homemaker. I have counseled clients who at seventy-five still feel like the incapable child of a now-deceased, hovering parent.

Beyond the disappointment of no longer living in the fantasy world of childhood lies the opportunity to become the adults who make real dreams come true, who create the family traditions and build new relationships. Although a part of me loved being a child, I must admit that I also was really glad to grow up. I remember feeling almost in prison by the many days and years I knew I would have to go to school. I remember the thrill of walking down Brattle Street during the spring of my senior year in college when I realized that the sixteen-year haul of school was about to be over, and I really could do whatever I chose to do. Beyond the weight of responsibility that adults carry, there is a great creative opportunity to become, to create, and to live freely. If we can remember the thrill of being grown up and take the choices carefully in hand, we may ultimately have more fun as adults than we ever did as children.

The book thus far has focused on staying grown up on our visits as adults to see our family of origin. But if we are to remain adults on our visits home, we must be sure we are also focusing on the primary task of this season of our lives: creating our own adult homes.

This transition can be particularly hard for singles, who sometimes seem to wait for marriage rather than adulthood to begin building their homes (not having a shower or wedding invitations to proclaim a date on which they begin home making). Yet as adults, whether married or single, with children or cats, we must respond seriously to the call of adulthood to create, not just come from, a home. Home implies not only a place but a family, composed of a circle of chosen friends with whom we share our lives most deeply. Being active homemakers not only gives us a foundation for standing strong when we visit our family of origin but also gives us compassion as we realize the challenges of this relational construction business.

Where Do We Hang the Stockings?

When we were first married, my husband and I usually went to my parents' home in Virginia for the Christmas holidays. My mother made a red corduroy stocking for each of her sons-in-law, with their names embroidered in white across the top to match the stockings for all the children in our family. Christmas morning we all gathered for breakfast before anyone could open a present (a little less impatiently than when we were young, dutifully obedient to the tradition). We added stockings for the first grandchildren as they arrived and made the circle a little bigger around the tree and table. The number of stockings got rather large for the small number of children, and the filling of them got to be a bit of a hassle, although we all did pitch in and help.

<table>
<tr><td>

for personal reflection

Describe a time, place, and situation that made you realize you were an adult with your own home base.

</td></tr>
</table>

At a certain point, I began to wonder how my children would remember Christmas. I realized that unless I wanted them to remember Christmas as a grandparents' holiday, I would have to stay at my own home and make my own Christmas traditions for my children. When my second son was born, I decided it was time. (The thought of trekking to Virginia with two small children and all the Christmas presents undoubtedly gave me courage to make the decision.) We would stay at our house for Christmas. I would be the adult cooking and wrapping and planning. Grandparents would be welcome to join us, or we would visit them another time, but it was time for me to make the holiday happen for our

169

marriage and our children. I would put away the "David" and "Anne" stockings and hang only our children's stockings from our mantel. I had grasped a piece of the baton for my lap of the race.

So my husband was right after all. The place I was living with him was my home. No longer could I claim the family vacation spot as my home. Though it might feel like scratchy new pants rather than the faded familiar jeans, the place I lived most of the time was where I must make home. When my young mother first hung those red corduroy stockings on her mantle years ago, it must have felt strange, too. Yet they grew strangely familiar over the years. Now I needed to begin making my home, which would become over the years worn, smooth, and familiar, too.

The shift looks different for each adult. I know couples who made the shift from squeezing in obligatory visits to both families on Christmas Day to declaring alternate years for each family to finally staying at their home for the holidays. My sister and her husband maintain their Christmas travels because it is a time with enough vacation from their work to visit family far away; but they make their own Thanksgiving with friends who are becoming family in their new locale. And they celebrate December in their home with an Advent-wreath making party every year. A single friend of mine whose family has moved and scattered throughout the years has worked to establish a traditional Christmas gathering of friends to serve international foods, sing Christmas carols, and play charades. Whether married or single, rich or poor, celebrating Christmas or Hanukkah, as adults we have the opportunity to choose and to create our own traditions and sense of family.

Sorting Wheat and Chaff

In the Museum of American Frontier Culture in my hometown of Staunton, Virginia, you can still try your hand with the huge old wooden fork that was used to toss the harvest to separate the wheat kernels from the stalks on which they grew. The nourishing wheat is kept while the rough chaff is thrown out. A tossing of our family harvest, sorting through those aspects of our family relationships and traditions that are kernels to keep and those stalks no longer needed, is a necessary starting place as we take up the task of building our own homes and families. We must decide what seeds to continue sowing

>
> *for personal reflection*
>
> *As you begin building your own traditions, you must sort through the wheat and chaff of your family harvest.*

and what new varieties of relationships to plant for the next season's harvest.

Recognizing the Kernels

First, ask yourself what aspects of your family home making that you most value and strongly wish to keep. What are the kernels of wheat that come from your mother and father, grandparents, aunts and uncles? Whether the harvest is full of wheat or the kernels are sparse, there is always something of value to be carefully replanted and continued into the next generation. Your wheat may be the qualities in relationships experienced in welcome-home hugs and talks regardless of success or failure, tough challenges for goal setting that press people to excellence, a mother and father's ability to ask for forgiveness that sets a tone of humility, or patient speaking of hope through times of trauma. Your kernels may be specific traditions you wish to pass on to children and grandchildren: making cinnamon rolls for the neighbors Christmas morning or singing "Cockle-de-do" after telling stories by the fire on family campouts or eating Irish soda bread on St. Patrick's day. From the quality of relationships to the little habits, think carefully about the gifts of your family that you wish to guard and maintain.

And then you must consider what the chaff is from your own family, those aspects you do not want to continue and pass on but rather sift out. The chaff may be alcohol that destroyed a wonderfully gifted person, anger that ruled a home from fear, caring that held so tight children felt smothered, valuing money over relationships, or being so cautious that courage was not tried. These patterns you wish to leave behind may take a lot of tossing and stomping to change, since they are deeply ingrained from living with them over years. Only with careful attention and work can you hope to leave them behind and replace them with new ways of being with one another.

My own sorting recently took physical form as I reconsidered Christmas stockings. Talking with my cousin about family traits, I realized with appreciation and humor that our childhood stockings were unusual in being made of corduroy. For my children I had chosen more decorative stockings but decided finally to revive the corduroy stockings in tribute to the family values of frugality and practicality. However, I would make them larger and add fancy gold trim and beaded decoration as my symbol of bounty and beauty at celebration times. They were first hung for my oldest son's sixteenth Christmas. In this case, sorting took a long time.

Fuel from Failures

Sometimes those people with the most painful memories are able to convert them into fuel for this hard family work, as the earth converts decomposing matter into oil. The son who grew up with his father's harsh anger uses it to catch himself when his patience grows thin with his own sons. The daughter who lived with a smothering mother uses the memory of that claustrophobic feeling to give her courage to travel the world. The woman who lived with abusive parents makes that motivation for attentive care to the details of her daughters' young lives. I have discovered that those whose family memories are most intensively bad are often those most intensely willing to work to make things better in their own families. They are the most focused in their efforts to parent carefully, most strong in their efforts to overcome the past. So if you feel you have lots of chaff, consider how it might be fuel for the home fires.

Rituals for Relationship

One way to help your wheat grow strong is to build a ritual around it. Rituals may be as simple as the good morning kiss on both checks to mother or the "You can do it!" cheer as a player begins a game. Or they can be as elaborate as the particular Seder dinner or Easter Eve celebration of light followed over the centuries. Rituals cement our values in physical actions and help build cohesion, stability, and tradition in our families. In research on faith develop-

for personal reflection

**What do you most
want to build in
your family?
Create a tradition
around it.**

ment in families, the presence of family rituals is one of the critical factors in a family's faith growth.

So think about what you most want to build in your family, especially perhaps those things you did not have in your own family growing up, and creatively imagine a ritual to cement it.

My husband grew up with perhaps only one family vacation. His father valued hard work, as he does, but found little time for adventure and fun. So my husband has made a priority of relationship rituals with our sons. Risings at 3:00 A.M. to go duck hunting in November are a must with each boy as he is old enough, and our youngest one has been treated to a father-son weekend after the hunting season is over.

As an adult, I began to value quiet time when people were not all talking or moving about, so we began an occasional quiet time together as a family. We turn out all the lights, light a candle, sing an introductory song, and take five minutes of silence together, after which we share on a bit more of a heart level our impressions or concerns. The ritual makes concrete the value of silence and listening, even while being with others. Specially developed rituals can help build into your life and relationships those values that you most treasure.

Creativity can help create rituals unique to your family with a flavor of fun. I know a busy family who found birthday dinners hard to keep. They developed instead their own ritual of birthday breakfasts with pancakes and candles. Another family that loves artichoke hearts celebrates any family success with an artichoke dinner.

Consider as well your way of handling the daily routines of life and see if you cannot consciously adopt newly modified patterns that are chosen to reflect your adult values. Think for example of dinner time. If you grew up with the TV as your discussion and everyone eating at different times, you might work hard to have family dinners—without TV or phone interruptions. On the other hand, you may have grown up with family meals so rigid that children were not allowed to voice their opinions. You may decide to keep regular meals together but be more flexible on manners and use the time together to encourage all to express their own ideas. One family in which the mother had become a short-order cook for everyone modified their routine by fixing a common menu and rotating who did the cooking, since the children were capable teens.

Rituals must be continually revisited to make sure they stay alive and true to family goals. The best rituals act as anchors through rough and smooth times yet have flexibility enough not to become dead weights. Two images help me in thinking about whether my rituals are becoming dead or continuing to bring life: Lenin's tomb and a snowball for a snowman.

Lenin's tomb stands in the heart of Red Square, which is at the heart of Moscow, which is at the heart of Russia. Lenin was a thinker whose ideas empowered a whole nation into a new way of living. When he died, his thoughts continued to fuel the nation in its growth as a communist state. His beginning ideas were considered and tried, worked and reworked, growing even after his death. Eventually they ceased to inspire and to work in that country. When I visited Moscow in 1991, the country was moving beyond Lenin and his communist ideals. Yet still his tomb was at the center of the square, guarded yet hardly visited except as a relic of the past. Lenin was dead and his tomb, once the center of inspiration, was now a symbol of what had not worked. I do not want my own family rituals that no longer work to sit in the middle of my living room or my holidays like Lenin's tomb, still visited but offering no inspiration.

On the other hand, I think of a snowball that begins as a rather small mound of snow. It keeps its center but gathers weight and shape with every layer of fresh snow that is added. Several such snowballs are layered on top of each other to make a snowman with its own particular character. Likewise, family traditions can begin as a simple idea but can be rolled over in their repetition in a way that gains weight and character with each use. Added to each other, such family traditions make up their own snowman, similar in basic outline but of a character unto themselves.

My extended family found itself a few years ago with a Lenin's tomb in our midst in the form of the Great Christmas Present Exchange. We had loved the eager anticipation and delight of Christmas morning gifts as children. As we grew, we learned to give to our parents and each other. As we each married and had children, we added these family members to our Christmas lists. By the time each of my parents' three children were married and had several children, buying, wrapping, and then mailing gifts became more of a tedious trial than an enjoyable experience. The giving of Christmas presents, meant to symbolize the great surprise of the free gift of God in Jesus, had turned into a materialistic, laborious, and largely lifeless duty. Finally, someone blew the whistle. Perhaps one of the wives finally heard the moaning or saw the eye rolling of their husbands. We decided to halt all the adult exchanges except for one gift by each person to one other person, drawn in a lottery. The dead body of Christmas duty was let go and simple surprise giving somewhat restored.

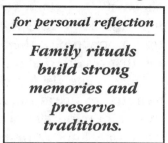

for personal reflection

Family rituals build strong memories and preserve traditions.

I have experienced the liturgy of the Episcopal family of worshipers in which I grew up to function at times like Lenin's tomb and at other times like a giant snowball. I grew up saying the word *propitiation* more times than spaghetti yet never knowing what it meant. The rite of worship that had been developed centuries earlier out of deep faith was for me an ordeal to be endured by playing with (and often dropping) pennies and singing an occasional familiar hymn. Without a personal living faith, the liturgy was fairly dead, though it was a Lenin's tomb that I faithfully visited.

I came to a deep personal faith apart from the Episcopal Church. But I remember vividly my first Christmas as a true believer standing awestruck by the liturgy that I had heard so many times before. Familiar words from Scripture leapt out at me. Its beauty and espression of deep faith amazed me. Because of my resentment that repeating these words had not been able to communicate that faith to me, I chose for many years to worship in fellowships of a more spontaneous variety. Eventually, though, I was drawn back to the liturgy when I was introduced to a vibrant use of it within a community of people who could talk about what the words meant personally. As I have rolled the words over my tongue from a starting point of faith, they, like a snowball, have increased in meaning with each rolling. And some rolls stay with me powerfully every time I now repeat them because of a spiritual moving that occurred at an earlier point.

Once while visiting New York City, I walked into a church service at 108th and Amsterdam. I took part in Communion with a very diverse group gathered early one Sunday morning in the city that never sleeps. As we repeated the words of thanks after eating bread and drinking wine, the words "heirs through hope" rang out and sank deep into my soul. Now every time I repeat that prayer I remember the gathered saints across the world with whom I am an heir through hope in that everlasting kingdom. Another Sunday, at the closing Eucharist of a woman's retreat, I experienced the transformation of a room by the tears of the woman priest that flowed upon the reading of the familiar opening prayer, "O Lord, unto whom all hearts are open . . ." Our hearts had been opened that weekend, and she freely cried at that graced realization, freeing us in turn to shed our tears. I have never since begun the liturgy with those words without a deep awareness of God's crying, loving eyes.

The liturgy is the ritual of the family of God. It can become more dead with each roll or come more alive and full. So, too, the rituals of our families. The lighting of the Sabbath candles, the choosing of the family Christmas tree, the cutting of the king's cake on Epiphany, the blessing before eating dinner, or the goodnight kiss—all can become dryer and duller or richer and fuller with our use. We must work to keep them full or make changes so that our home making continues to grow with life.

Thanksgiving has been my family's most successful snowball holiday as we have added layers of ritual and enjoyment with the years. Thanksgiving began with little more tradition than a big turkey dinner with my parents if we were able to make it to their house. As we all had children, there were more people around for the holiday, making no one house large enough for the gathering. Yet we all wanted to see each other, so a common Thanksgiving feast at a neutral large gathering spot was instituted. Everyone brought a favorite dish, many of which became hits with family members. No one had to slave over a hot stove all day or clean up on their own, and the more the merrier could be the rule. As my boys got older, the combination of hunt and cousin gathering made Virginia the only possible option for them. Then I added a layer to the family ritual when I decided to join the hunt. The first year I hunted early on Thanksgiving Day with my husband and sons and we all went out for breakfast after that—another tradition established! One tradition has built on another to make it a holiday that has grown with the years and the particulars of family preferences.

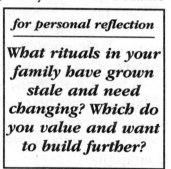

for personal reflection

What rituals in your family have grown stale and need changing? Which do you value and want to build further?

Consider your own family rituals. Which rituals do you value in your family of origin and, as with snowballs, want to keep rolling over in your own home so they gain in weight and character? Which are valuable but have become cumbersome and need modifying? Which have grown stale or dead like Lenin's tomb and need to be let go? Finally, think anew of the values you hold—as a couple, as a family, as your own self. What are ways to build new rituals that will express and uphold them?

Parents in Process

Although we are the adults now and this is our lap, a word of caution is in order. We are never wise enough and capable enough when we become parents. As humans, we are either young and filled with energy but not wisdom or we are old and wise but without energy to keep up. A most important characteristic for parents is to stay in process, to keep learning and growing. There is no harder or hotter crucible for showing up weaknesses and bringing one's own needs to the surface than being a parent. Children know their parents all too well. And that means parents can learn from their children about their own strengths and weaknesses and use that to keep growing.

I have observed several sorts of grandparents. Usually, good parents become even better grandparents, often loving that role even more than parenting. Then there are those who were not the greatest parents. They were too harsh with the kids, had a bad temper, were away too much, or nagged too often. But they learned from their mistakes and mellowed, so that by the time they became grandparents they were really pretty good at grandparenting. They matured through life and accepted the parenting process as one of learning for themselves. A final type are those people who believe they are the wizards and stay rigid in their ways, not learning from their faults or laughing at their ineptness. As they age and become grandparents, they become harder and more difficult than ever. They become more and more fake wizards rather than parents who stay in process and grow into wise old folks.

Henri Nouwen, a Dutch priest who grew old with wisdom to share with others, encouraged people to aim not for success in their lives but for fruitfulness. When we do, we become homemakers who are truly "generative," growing through the generations.

"These Are the Good Old Days"

I remember my grandparents talking about the days of their growing up. Somehow in my mind, those were always "the good old days." The good old days were the days of fond memories, fun, and adventure. For those too old to still go on such adventures, talking about memories filled empty days and shared history with the next generation. One day in my thirties, I had a sudden realization that the days I was living then were what I would one day call my "good old days." It was a frightening thought because I was not finding them all that good. I was going crazy with too many meals to make, errands to run, phone calls to return, and projects to complete. I realized that if I was not enjoying these so-called prime and best years of my life I was in trouble. So I decided to slow down enough to be aware of what I was doing. I worked to appreciate the breeze on my face as I walked into my son's school to volunteer, the opportunity to share deeply with a person in crisis in my office, even the plates which had been filled with food that I was now washing. Since then, I regularly try to remind myself, in the words of a song, "These are the good old days." I still sometimes let a day or many days go by without stopping to just be thankful for the day, but when I realize they have passed in a fog, I chastise myself and make a renewed effort to slow down. These are the days I was waiting to grow up into, and I'd better enjoy the lap as I'm running.

Keep an Eye on Yourself

As you go home to visit family, keep your observer eyes open, not only to see your family patterns and your part in them but also the wheat and chaff that you wish to sort for your tough job of creating family. When we are old enough to be assessing our parents, we are old enough to be home making as well. As we try that hard task, we will need all the fuel from both strong foundations and failure, all the creativity of our inner selves, and plenty of grace when we stumble in order to keep running and growing.

Epilogue

As I was beginning to write this book, I recognized that I would have to do some of my own home-going work if I was to write genuinely and call others to this heartfelt home making. So, as I was preparing for my visit home last summer, I dutifully followed the basic steps for relationship preparation, hoping at least to gain a few helpful illustrations in the process. What transpired were dramatic family developments that I never would have foreseen. Usually, small steps lead to small results (or even great resistance) in families. Occasionally, taking what seems to be a small step forward to be truly yourself in your family will set off reverberations that result in mammoth changes for relationships within the extended family. That is what has happened, quite unexpectedly, to me over the course of the last year.

While I was packing bathing suits, walking shoes, and shorts for my trip home last summer, I considered what I wanted during the visit. One thing stood out as that which nourishes my soul most: time viewing the sunset and sunrise on the mountain ridge at the family farm. So, I planned my trip almost selfishly, not giving up a sunset to stay over with my parents the first night or to greet my sister the second night but arranging as much time on the land as possible. In former visits my performing of the expected role of being with family would have prevented my carving out this individual time. On Saturday morning I rose very early for a night watch, as I had every Saturday for three years as a spiritual Sabbath quiet time. I sat in the midst of dew-laden grass on the hilltop watching the black sky turn to the darkest blue, then royal, and baby blue, and then waiting for the neon ball to appear out of the morning fog over the Blue Ridge Mountains. In my soul, I suddenly grasped the bone-deep love of this land my grandfather had had, as if it had been thrown across the generations on this mysterious morning. And he, as if along with the pioneers and ancient Native Americans, along with the Creator, called to me in this place. As I rose to walk, my mind was filled with the vision of being here more often, complete with floor plans of a family retreat house. I treasured these moments secretly in my heart, and went on with the day.

Later that afternoon, while preparing horses in the barn for the children to ride, my cousin reflected on how our grandfather always was making things happen. She lamented that not too much had happened on the farm the last number of years. I asked what she might wish and imagine next, and she said they wanted to sell the logs from the hay barn in order to rebuild the deteriorating horse stable. When I heard *logs* and *sell*, I knew I must tell her of my morning's vision. One thing quickly led to another, and by the next day, my husband had handed her a check for the logs as her starter money for rebuilding the stable and the first timber for my yet-to-be-fleshed-out dream. Thus began a year of the two of us cousins together envisioning the building of this farm for the next generation—as a place refurbished with horses to ride and a retreat house for family and friends. As we took the lead, her parents and mine, our brothers and sisters, and all the children joined in support of our seemingly crazy idea. The logs came down, a new stable roof was raised over new plank walls. And a one-room hermitage rose up with the help and almost miraculous weaving together of building details.

I sat amidst remnants of stove pipe and floor planks in this almost completed hermitage while I read the final edit of this book, amazed that the year of writing about going home turned into a year of my family transformation as well. I discovered that by bringing my adult determination to be true to what I treasured on my trips home, I ultimately gained vision and energy that is allowing me to return home much more often. Undoubtedly, ongoing family growth will be much slower and more laborious than this particular chapter of my family history, and occasionally I will experience deeply disappointing setbacks. But my hope is that those who pursue the steps in this book, along with the tedious work and difficulties, will also find surprises in store. I imagine these might come in forms as diverse as a renewed relationship to an aunt, a discovery of a mother's hidden artistic talent that resonates with one's own, a satisfaction with one's ability to leave a holiday not devastated, or a father-son whitewater expedition that becomes a family tradition.

This book and this past year have taught me most personally that when we are honest and true to ourselves, we pave the way for genuine rather than robotic relationships. My hope is that as we put forth reflection, planning, and work, we will find the relationships—the greatest valuables of our visits—increasingly polished and enjoyable.

Notes

1. *Mothers Who Love Too Much* (New York: Fawcett Columbine, 1988) is my book written particularly for these families.

2. If you wish to do further family exploration, a helpful resource is Monica McGoldrick's *You Can Go Home Again* (New York: Norton, 1995). This book introduces the family therapists' tool of *genograms,* which, like a family tree, help you to map out your family. This can lead to great personal growth and a much better understanding of how your family operates. A simpler and quite practical guide to understanding your family is Dr. Ronald Richardson's *Family Ties That Bind* (Seattle: Self-Counsel Press, 1984).

3. See Lewis Smedes's *Forgive and Forget* (San Francisco: Harper, 1996) for a more in-depth exploration of forgiveness.

4. My story of this time is a chapter in *Women's Spiritual Passages,* ed. Lucinda McDowell (Wheaton, Ill.: Shaw, 1996).

5. All proceeds from the sale of this book will be contributed to Amistad Mission to support their parenting of these abandoned children, who now have only the adoptive parents of the mission. For further information, you may write Amistad Mission, P.O. Box 12183, Birmingham, AL 35202-2183.

6. Dennis Linn, Sheila Fabricant, and Matthew Linn, *Sleeping with Bread* (New York: Paulist Press, 1995).